Praise for *How to Tell Stories to Children*

"I wish I'd read this book before my children grew up. Its simple insights and practices will make me a better storyteller."
- Charles Eisenstein, Author of *The More Beautiful World Our Hearts Know is Possible*

"The book is well written and deftly conveys its lessons to readers, avoiding preachiness as it argues that storytelling is a way to provide kids with the attention they crave. The authors are encouraging throughout, making a solid case for storytelling as a skill that can be developed by anyone and practiced effectively by amateurs. Readers. will walk away from the book feeling empowered and capable. The sample tales do a fine job of demonstrating how children can be satisfied by simple narratives, and the exercises ("Find Something Small and Make It Big"; "Change Your Voice") deliver guidance while inspiring readers to experiment. An informative and practical guide for adults who want to be successful storytellers."
- Kirkus Reviews

"This isn't really a book about technique. It peels away technical concerns and takes you to the glowing heart of the matter: telling stories to children is a bonding, nurturing, embracing and thoroughly natural thing for any adult to do. Silke and Joe invite you to claim your rich human legacy and experience the joy and satisfaction of telling stories, any stories, to the children in your life."
- Joe Hayes, Professional Storyteller

"I believe this kind of practical wisdom is what fathers and mothers need to connect with their children in a spiritual, loving, and easily effective way. Frankly, it is probably much better than just sending them to church."
- Fr. Richard Rohr, *New York Times* Bestselling Author and Founder of the Center for Action and Contemplation

"I love this book! Stories give us ways to connect and consider what we have in common with each other, and to celebrate what makes us delightfully different."
- Melanie DeMore, African-American Folk Singer & Storyteller

"After 40 years of teaching, training teachers, and even longer in telling stories - this is the first book I've seen quite like this."
- Sara Tisdel, Teacher & Teacher-Trainer

"What a great idea for a book! Humans understand the world primarily through stories, which means you can shape the world of the small people you love with just a bit of fancy and a lot of love."
- Bill McKibben, Environmentalist and *New York Times* Bestselling Author of *The End of Nature*

"In these times of relational poverty, daily stress, and trauma, storytelling is an accessible modality for any parent, teacher or counselor that promotes connection, hope, healing and resiliency— and Silke and Joe provide this important gift through their original stories, ancestral tales and teachings."
- Kara Andresen, LCSW, Child Therapist

"In this elegantly written guide, the authors – both gifted teachers of small children – reclaim the timeless tradition of storytelling, giving us practical tools for transforming the most ordinary life experiences into magical adventures to captivate and engage listeners of all ages."
- Mirabai Starr, Author of *Caravan of No Despair* and *Wild Mercy*

"With every chapter, I felt inspired. I began trusting in the moment, not knowing where the story would take us."
- Jenny Sue Kostecki-Shaw, Children's Author and Illustrator of *Same, Same but Different*

How To Tell Stories to Children

to Children

Silke Rose West
Joseph Sarosy

Cover art by Jenny Kostecki-Shaw.
ISBN: 978-0-578-55027-5

To the Earth Children

"Unreal beliefs in unseen forces…are much more likely to motivate action than are modestly real beliefs."

Brian Boyd, *On the Origin of Stories*

CONTENTS

# Introduction

Storytelling is one of the oldest and most intimate skills on the planet. Modern stories are big business, often told through movies, books and video games, but the oral tradition has something unique to offer – a lasting bond between storyteller and listener. It's a vital tool for parents, educators and anyone interested in a meaningful relationship with children, and there's a big difference between telling someone else's story and one of your own.

Think of it as the difference between a can of tomato sauce and homemade marinara. A practiced storyteller draws upon the events and objects within a child's immediate surroundings, like plucking tomatoes and herbs from the garden, then crafts stories that are not only entertaining (and tasty), but created precisely for those children in that place.

In this book, we outline the key ingredients for intuitive storytelling so that you can begin improvising your own stories directly from within the environment in which you and your children live. We are parents and teachers with hundreds, perhaps thousands, of story-hours under our belts, but this book has nothing to do with how to tell our stories, or anyone else's. It has everything to do with how to tell yours.

Silke (*silk-uh*) is a Waldorf teacher who has taught kindergarten for over thirty years. In 1995, she cofounded the Taos Waldorf School and today she runs an independent forest kindergarten called Taos Earth Children. She is renowned in Taos for her puppet shows and storytelling, and consults with teachers and schools nationally. Joe worked with Silke for two years at Taos Earth Children, and in 2018 he formed a loosely collaborative 1st grade, a multi-age group of children he plans to teach through the 8th grade. They are now in their second year of formation. Joe is also the author of *A Father's Life*, a book of stories about his time in nature with children, a finalist in the 2019 NIEA Awards. In 2018, he created the #Greatdad Campaign to highlight great fathers across the nation. A contributing writer for *Fatherly*, he has also written articles for the *Kosmos Journal* and writes a successful blog at offgridkids.org.

For both of us, storytelling is a principal part of our day. Our school days are largely spent outside, learning from within the local environment in which we live. Our stories are often about animals and plants, an upcoming holiday, or a craft we just made with the kids. Characters frequently encounter situations that the kids have recently seen themselves, including sticky classroom subjects and occasional behavior issues. At the end of story time, it is not uncommon for the kids to erupt with phrases like, "that was the best story ever!"

It's true that we're good storytellers, but what's much more critical is the emotional bond and shared experience we have with the kids, and the fact that our stories are crafted from events and objects they recognize. When we approach storytelling from this perspective, the goal is not to create the world's most engrossing narrative, but the day to day stories that build intimacy and trust between teacher (or parent) and child.

There are hundreds of storybooks available today, including several that give some instruction and background on storytelling. Some of these books are excellent, but each is primarily focused on memorizing or retelling stories that someone else created. This is not the intention of our book. What you hold in your hands is not a collection of stories. It is a method to help you craft your own.

The technique is simple, something we employ every day with a lot of variety and flexibility. Much of it stems from expert advice and academic research. However, the only expertise required is emotional contact with your children, something that you do better than anyone else.

Contrast this with the message from storyteller Marie Shedlock in the introduction to her classic *The Art of the Storyteller*, " It is to be hoped that someday stories will be told to school groups only by experts who have devoted special time and preparation to the art of telling them."

Shedlock means well, but this is precisely the opposite of our message. Everyone is a good storyteller and no expert can replace the intimacy of a story crafted from within a child's own environment by an attentive and loving parent or caregiver. Why? Because storytelling is about the relationship, not the narrative.

The intuitive method we describe in this book employs a simple architecture, starting with the physical objects and activities within your child's immediate environment. Sometimes, this can be as complicated as reframing a conflict among the children in the guise of a quarrel amongst squirrels, but often it's as simple as noticing a child's bare feet, then telling a story about what happened when her shoelaces took a walk down to the stream. Such stories make the kids giggle, and think. They feel like they are a part of it, because they recognize the characters and events in the stories from their real lives. They feel seen.

But that's not all. Because intuitive stories are crafted from within a child's environment, there is a direct and physical outlet for play afterward. This is the storytelling loop we describe in chapter one. It is not hard to imagine, for example, what a barefoot child who has recently heard a story about her shoelaces will do once she finds her shoes.

As a whole, the chapters in this book describe the ingredients of our storytelling method, but each topic is self -contained, so that most folks will have no trouble cherry picking. Each chapter can be read in less than ten minutes and is followed by a sample story to illustrate the advice given in that chapter. Many folks will find it easy to read the entire book in one sitting, but it would be perfectly suitable, and very much to our liking, if you read a chapter, try a story with your kids, then return another day for another tip. We've included practice exercises in each chapter to help you get started. Good storytelling, despite what Marie Shedlock says, is not about perfection. It's about practice. There is no rush.

We trust this method because we use it almost every day. We've seen it work in multiple settings over many years, and there is enormous flexibility. The framework is helpful, especially if you are just getting started, but no two stories and no two storytellers are ever the same. Good stories, like good people, are as diverse as the peaks of a mountain range, with all the valleys and streams between. Find your place. Find your voice. Your stories will be most fruitful when you stop listening to advice and simply follow the story that is already inside you.

If this book can be reduced to one message, it's this: *You are already a good storyteller*. It's literally what makes you human. It comes with the package, just like hair and opposable thumbs. So remember, if it's marinara you're after, make it yourself, and try a few different recipes the first time around. It will help, and it won't take long to beat the canned variety. But once you've mastered your particular taste, throw out the recipe book. Your intuition will take you and your kids further than you ever dreamed.

The Science Behind the Story

"…why, in a world of necessity [do] we choose to spend so much time caught up in stories that both teller and told know never happened and never will?"[1] This is the opening question of evolutionary theorist Brian Boyd's *On the Origin of Stories*. A similar question can be found in the pages of David Sloan Wilson's *Darwin's Cathedral*. Distinguished Professor of Biology and Anthropology at Binghamton University, Wilson has received countless awards for his work and recently received funding from the National Science Foundation to expand his evolutionary studies program into a national consortium. Is it possible, he asks, that cultural stories (in this case, specifically religious stories) unite their listeners into a group with distinct evolutionary advantages?[2]

The scope of these questions is well beyond the material tackled in *How to Tell Stories to Children* (we're just kindergarten teachers!). Nevertheless, the emerging conversation among cognitive researchers, neuroscientists and evolutionary theorists sheds a tremendous amount of light on the gravity of storytelling and it's worth opening a small window into that world.

Put simply, we are an extraordinarily social species, sometimes labeled super-social. The success we have gained as a species, and therefore as individuals, is due in large part to our ability to cooperate (and compete) with one another. The thin line we tread between cooperation and competition with our family, clan and neighbors has driven the development of remarkable tools to share information, withhold information, read the intentions of others, and impress or conceal our own intentions upon them.

One of those principal tools is storytelling. Storytelling is how we tell people what happened, what we wish had happened, or what we'd like to do now. Jennifer Aaker, professor of marketing at the Stanford Graduate School of Business, reports that people remember information when it is incorporated into a narrative "up to 22 times more than facts alone."[3] Stories are also the principal method we use to mislead, or attempt to mislead, others with lies. Put on the spot, most four-year-olds will spontaneously fabricate stories to avoid uncomfortable truths.[4] Adults aren't much better. Gossip amounts to nearly 65% of all communication in public.[5]

But stories are more, much more, than a means of conveying truths or deceptions. They are, as we know from billion-dollar movies, bestselling books, and 30,000 year old cave paintings, one of the most engrossing activities for human beings everywhere. We pay money for a good story, even though, as Brian Boyd states incisively, "both teller and told know [it] never happened and never will." Why?

Beyond the simple measures of truth-telling or deception, human beings use stories to garner attention, simulate actions (including emotions), and develop trust. Storytelling is the primary way we pass values between members of our social group, including from parent to child. " Stories," states a recent article in the *Atlantic*, "can be a way for humans to feel that we have control over the world. They allow people to see patterns where there is chaos...a form of existential problem-solving."[6]

Perhaps now we can begin to understand why David Sloan Wilson suggests that cultural and religious stories might hold an evolutionary advantage for their listeners. Cooperation among community members, Wilson says, has always been a vital component of human survival. "Loving and serving a perfect god," however, "is vastly more motivating than loving and serving one's imperfect neighbor." In other words, "A fictional belief system that is user-friendly and that motivates an adaptive suite of behaviors will surpass a realistic belief system that requires a Ph.D. to understand." It's important to recognize that Wilson is not suggesting that religious beliefs are fictional (or true), merely that, whether true or not they are deeply imbued with stories that motivate behavior.

Most parents observe this on a daily basis. Whether a recent Harry Potter book or a Disney movie, children tend to act and speak out the stories they have recently heard, read or watched. Adults do much the same, repeating the best lines from our favorite movies, and even taking on some of the flamboyance of our favorite characters.

Storytelling is the principal method by which we pass culture (or meaning) from parent to child and human to human. And not just meaning, but ways of being. Poise. Tone. Swagger. Family history. Storytelling is also, along with touch, one of the greatest arbiters of intimacy and trust. People who frequently share stories are usually bonded in unique and lasting ways. This is why *Psychology Today* lists it as their number one recommendation to parents interested in raising a happy child.[7] The content is almost inconsequential. The emotional intimacy is what we crave, and it turns out that sharing stories builds it better than almost anything.

In his influential book *The Storytelling Animal*, Jonathan Gottschall writes that fiction, "will make you more empathic and better able to navigate life's dilemmas."[8] Stories, he says, are like dress rehearsals for real life. He quotes Marco Iacoboni, a pioneering neuroscientist at UCLA who studies mirror neurons: "We have empathy for fictional characters...because we literally experience the same feelings ourselves." Storytelling is not an evolutionary glitch, Gottschall concludes, "fiction is...good for us."

Our hope is that this book will inspire you to claim the tradition of storytelling for yourself. It is your birthright as a human being, and none of this academic jargon is required. In fact, you are already telling stories throughout much of your day, whether to yourself, at the office, or in a circle of friends. Gottschall says it well, "story is for a human as water is for a fish." You have the tools. You have the history. By stepping consciously into this role with your child, you repeat a journey millions of parents and caregivers have taken before. With practice, you might even discover that you are an exceptional storyteller, but this much is certain – the emotional bond that naturally arises from storytelling will be a lasting gift for you and your child.

[1]Boyd, B. (2009). *On the Origin of Stories*. Cambridge, MA: Belknap Press.

[2]Wilson, D. S. (2003). *Darwin's Cathedral*. Chicago, IL: University of Chicago Press.

[3]Aaker, J. (2014). *Lean In: Harnessing the Power of Stories* [Video file]. Retrieved from https://leanin.org/education/harnessing-the-power-of-stories

[4]Vitelli, R. (2013, November 11). When Does Lying Begin. Retrieved from https://www.psychologytoday.com/us/blog/media-spotlight/201311/when-does-lying-begin

[5]Healy, B. (2018, July). Gossiping is Good. Retrieved from https://www.theatlantic.com/magazine/archive/2018/07/gossip-is-good/561737/#4

[6]Delistraty, C. (2014, November 2). The Psychological Comforts of Storytelling. Retrieved from https://www.theatlantic.com/health/archive/2014/11/the-psychological-comforts-of-storytelling/381964/

[7]Allyn, P. (2013, July). 10 Ways to Raise a Happy Child. Retrieved from https://www.psychologytoday.com/us/blog/litlife/201307/10-ways-raise-happy-child

[8]Gottschal, J. (2012). *The Storytelling Animal*. New York, NY. Houghton Mifflin Harcourt Publishing Co.

The Storytelling Loop

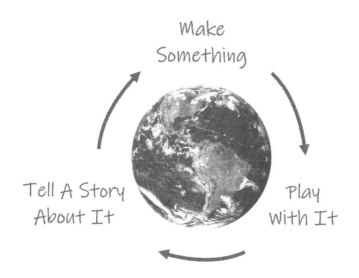

Make
Something

Tell A Story
About It

Play
With It

Here's how it works — make a fairy boat from twigs and grass. Or noodles, computer parts or scraps of carpet. Whatever. Then, let the kids play with it. It doesn't even matter if it sinks. Just laugh. Later, after lunch or during a quiet time, tell a story about a mouse (or a fairy, an ant, etc.) who finds a small boat and sets sail for adventure.

Don't have a fairy boat? Make a little house or a fort. You can refer to a child's backpack, a discarded piece of gum, or a tree with a unique crook in its branches. Anything. Take one to three concrete things (or events) from your day and use them as anchors in your story.

This technique ties reality into imagination, then back again. Afterward, the kids will probably want to play out some of the story, in which case they might need a boat. This is the storytelling loop – a real situation, imaginary development, followed by a new real situation – and it comes in all shapes and sizes. We might represent it like this.

The Storytelling Loop

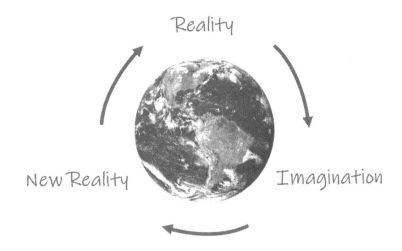

A beginning storyteller will usually start with simple whimsical stories, but a practiced storyteller begins to see loops in all sorts of situations, like a group of bickering children. They can be reprimanded, of course, but it is often more effective to tell a story. United by the common story, rather than pinpointed in their division, children have the opportunity to regroup as a team to act out the story. A real event transformed by story into a new reality.

Here's another one. A child has an aching tooth. Witnessing a child's pain can be excruciating for parents. We take them to the dentist and give them medicine, but some things, like new molars, can't be doctored away. So, we give them an ice cube and tell a story. It's about a child with an aching tooth who got so fed up she went on a journey to heal her pain. Along the way she met a beaver, who had to chew incessantly because his teeth never stopped growing. "Think you got pain?" he said, perhaps a little rudely. He even chewed wood while he talked. Then came an elephant who was sad and sympathetic. "Growing tusks," she said, "was one of the most painful experiences of my life." There was a crocodile, who was a little snappy, a shark, even a saber-toothed tiger. Each of them had a different personality, a word of comfort, or just a grump. Finally, the wandering child met an old miner deep in a cave, a tiny gnome, who harvested teeth for the tooth fairy. "Those molars," he said, "are tough work. I have to climb way up a child's nose and push and pull till they come down. No wonder they hurt."

None of this will change the pain in a child's jaw, but if spoken with a sympathetic word and maybe a touch of humor, she might walk away with a little more resolve. Again, this is the storytelling loop – the transformation of a real event into one with more meaning. It is an incomparable tool for parents.

The storytelling loop is a journey we take with the kids. Sometimes it lasts hours. At others, just a few minutes. Often it's just for fun (and that's usually the best place for beginners), but as your craft develops, you will find it surprisingly easy to include deeper and deeper levels of meaning. After all, what are the Gospels or the Vedas if not stories?

There are plenty of ways to begin and end your story in the imaginative world, but in this book we focus on taking an object or event from the real world into your narrative with you. By doing so, we help our children (and ourselves) bridge reality and imagination. In time, you might no longer need this strategy, but if you're just beginning to tell stories, you'll find that this simple practice opens up a rich source of material for exploration on both sides – reality and imagination. Story is the bridge.

Think of the journey – over the bridge and back again – as one loop. If we threaded a needle and brought it with us, we might find that we had made a stitch between reality and imagination. A practiced storyteller has made hundreds of such stitches in the fabric of reality. She has dozens of bridges, and she places them carefully, choosing locations that are appropriate for her child's age and her family's values. A child who has accompanied her on these journeys has no trouble crossing the bridge himself. He is continually weaving a dense fabric of imagination into the very real places and things in his home, his neighborhood, his town. He has ignited a curiosity that will last a lifetime. Such a child sees doors in even the most mundane of objects. You will too.

One of the reasons this storytelling method is successful is that it requires little preparation. Methods that require memorization or preparation, well-meaning as they are, can be difficult for parents and teachers who lack the time or motivation to follow through. Similarly, if a storyteller tries to predict or prepare the end of a story during the telling, there's a good chance he will find himself distracted and the story will fizzle. The key to simple, effortless storytelling is to remain present and let the story flow.

In other words, we're not looking for a script, a beginning or an end. We might not even have a clear sense of what the story will look like. We're simply crossing a bridge, a curious bridge, and watching the story unfold in our own imaginations. When it ends, we close the loop, bringing the story back to reality and allowing a simple outlet for play.

The bridge we take is commonly an object from within our child's environment. This might be a toy, but it could also be a place, or a butterfly. Whatever it is, make sure it's something that caught *your* attention too. You are an important part of the story, and we don't want to lose you.

For example, we might be sitting on a hillside playing in the grass with a few dolls. At the bottom of the hill, a small creek runs by. During a quiet moment, perhaps after lunch, we might tell a story about one of those dolls who, when no one was looking, walked down to the creek for a swim. Here, the doll is the bridge, and the story easily proceeds without foreknowledge or preparation. What does it feel like for the doll to walk? Is she slow and careful? Stealthy and sharp? Is she a bit of a bumbler? Does she trip and fall into the water with a big splash? What kinds of things does she see? As the telling proceeds from one event to another, you watch the doll stroll through your imagination. What does she do when she gets to the water's edge? It's up to you, and the character of the moment.

For some this might feel a bit forced, but there is a moment when the story takes hold of the teller. It's as if we're walking across the bridge, not exactly sure where we're going, sort'a scratching our heads, when all of a sudden we get a glimpse of the other side, make a wide smile, and begin to run. *I want that doll on a boat with a crab.* This is what we're looking for, not a memorized narrative, because from there on out the story drives itself. The teller has sunk fully into his imagination and is no longer distracted. His excitement becomes the child's excitement. It hardly matters where the story goes or ends. When it does end, your child will have a new window into her doll. She may want to reenact the story. She might need a crab. Or maybe she wants to take the doll on a new adventure. That's the juice that we're looking for.

We might also find a bridge in an activity, like a child jumping rope. In this case, we might tell a story about an ant that loved to jump rope and a caterpillar that came along to join her. When you think of an ant jumping rope, what comes to mind? What about a caterpillar? He might have a hard time getting all those legs to jump at the same time. Simple stories like this can infuse a dull afternoon with new excitement. The ensuing play might just be a return to the jump rope with a new giggle. It might be the reenactment of the caterpillar jumping over the rope one foot at a time. You might have to build a giant life-size caterpillar.

The subsequent play after a story is just an option. It's not something we force, or even encourage. The story simply allows it. A path for play is opened up, but it is up to the children to choose whether they take it. If storytelling becomes a regular routine, one will see how frequently stories turn into playtime, and vice versa. This is the magic of the storytelling loop. But it will not be every time, and it's important to give the children the freedom of their own choice. It's also important to accept that some of your stories will be duds. There's nothing wrong with that.

The examples in this chapter are mostly whimsical, because this is where most people will start. The intimacy that is generated through these simple stories will, in time, allow some storytellers to find bridges in more complicated moments, such as an injury, a difficult social encounter, or the death of a loved one. Later chapters will tackle this material, but here is a middle of the road example.

Imagine a child who frequently leaves his jacket behind, whether at school, in the park, at a friend's house, etc. It's easy to get frustrated with such a child and admonish him to remember. He sheepishly promises to do better, but he never does, and it begins to be a sore point between child and parent.

Let's use the jacket as a bridge, and turn it into a story about a bear who went swimming and unzipped his fur coat. He left it on the shore, then forgot and was embarrassed when he got home naked. Maybe winter came and he had to go on a great search, only to find that a few squirrels and a rabbit had made a tent out of it. Such stories make the kids laugh, and gently but effectively send home the message without singling any one of them out for criticism. The jacket may still get left behind, but now we have a literary device that defuses the tension. "Hey! Don't be a naked bear!" becomes a funny, kind way to remind so-and-so to get his jacket. Such stories bring parent and child together, rather than dividing them into problem and criticizer.

Practice #1 – Simply Observe

Start looking at your child's environment for bridges into storyland. These might be toys, activities, places, or food. What excites you, or makes you laugh? Be honest. The examples in this chapter included fairies, dolls, and bugs, but you might find ninja turtles or computer games more exciting. Whatever catches your attention, try to see them as bridges, or doors, into storyland. Where might you like to see them go?

Sample Story – The Metal Pipe Gnome

By Joseph Sarosy

I was sitting in the passenger seat. A friend was driving down the two-lane highway while our daughters, five and six, sat in the back looking at a picture book. We had been on the road for thirty minutes already, and it would be a good bit longer before we reached our destination. A few parents and kids sat in other cars front and back of us. Our entire kindergarten class was carpooling to Farmer Ron's, eager to see his orchards and fields once again.

But the going was slow. The installation of a major gas line made it so that the two-lane road, with a majestic view of the Rio Grande on our right, was occasionally reduced to one lane. Flaggers were posted every so often, and as we sat behind a stack of cars, we watched men in orange vests and yellow machines lift huge steel pipes into place.

"Dad, I'm bored..." said my friend's daughter, throwing the book on the floor. "Will you tell us a story?"

"Well...um..." my friend hedged. It was obvious from the first syllable that he didn't have one. Stories. Where do they come from? If you could just pluck them from a branch...

I listened patiently as my friend and his daughter bargained back and forth for a couple minutes, the whining and discomfort escalating as the car idled. I sat silently, trying to be polite. As it grew clear that a story was not forthcoming from my friend, I ventured an interruption. "I'll tell you what," I offered, "I'll tell you guys a story. But I have one rule..."

"What?"

"You can't enjoy it."

The girls laughed. My friend snickered. In case any confusion reigned, my daughter spoke up. "He just says that," she said, shaking her head, "it's not true."

"You're not true," I quipped. She rolled her eyes. I love this game.

"Alright," I began, "you know how Silke always tells stories about gnomes?"

"Yes..."

I had had a few moments to eye my surroundings as my friend bargained with his daughter. I didn't have a fairy boat, or a moss-covered castle. I didn't even have a plastic doll. But I did have metal pipes. Miles of 'em. Everywhere you looked the earth was torn. Men in hard hats carried rakes and shovels, drove machines, and aimed plasma torches at huge steel pipes to weld them in place. Not exactly paradise, but it's what we had.

"Well," I said, as yet not knowing the story I was about to tell, "one gnome was on his way to Taos." I began to picture him, a stubby little guy with a pointy hat. " He was walking along the road, this road, and he was coming to help people get ready for Christmas." Silke had told us about these guys earlier, called wichtels actually, but I'll spare you the German history lesson.

Apparently, they help with little tasks around the holidays, like chopping wood and cleaning hearths. The girls knew this, and the fact that gnomes shouldn't be seen.

"He was walking along the edge of the road, sticking to the grasses and bushes to stay hidden, when he came to a huge pile of mud. Really just a mess. There were pipes and machines everywhere and all kinds of tools and stuff. Fortunately, it was the weekend, so all the workers were home. They were probably getting ready for Christmas..."

The long procession of cars coming from the opposite direction finally stopped, and the pilot car, having made a three-point turn, began to drive back the other way. The flagger in front of us turned his sign around, from stop to slow, and we started inching forward.

"Well, the gnome started walking through all this mess and it was really slow going. He had to climb up muddy hills and there wasn't a lot of grass to hide behind, so he had to run from machine to machine. And, well, it was a lot of work.

"At one point, a car came screaming around the corner and he had to hide quick. But there was nowhere to go. He looked left. He looked right. Then, spying the huge metal pipe above him, he hopped inside."

The girls giggled. My friend snorted. To be honest, till then, I wasn't really sure where the story was going. I was just kind of saying things till I found my footing. But now that I had a gnome in a giant metal pipe, I began to smile. I could feel the story.

"Well, it was dark in there," I said, growing more comfortable. "He looked around, trying to get his bearings, but he couldn't make anything out." *By now, we were sailing smoothly in the car.* "Finally, he heard something." *I paused, as if listening for it.* "Dink. Dink. Pink, ponk, pink... *It was hard to tell what it was, but it sounded like tiny scraps of metal hitting each other, or like... like... a fork falling on the floor.* Pink, ponk, pink...

"It was everywhere. *The noises came from every direction and seemed to fill the entire pipe.* Pink. Donk. Dinky-dook... *The gnome started to get a little scared, but then he saw something. A light came on." I paused.*

Blackness. Small magic things inside real things we cannot see. A light comes on. Before I tell the girls what was in there, I'd like to ask — what do you see? What did the girls see? This is what we're after. There were four people in that car, but each saw with her own eyes. The story was now tied to the real world, which we saw plainly with our real eyes, but it also called forth creativity and vision from within each individual. Plus, it was tying us together as a band of four. This is the magic of storytelling.

"There, in the distance," I said, "the gnome began to make something out. *It wasn't one something, it was many of them. It was... well, maybe it was hundreds of them. Thousands.* Dink, donk, dink. *As they approached, the gnome saw that they were* hundreds of tiny little machines. They were the same color as the pipe, almost as if they had formed out of it, tiny robots with little wheels, arms and spindles. One had a giant drill for an arm and one had a little plasma welder. Suddenly, one formed into a bulldozer, pushed aside some scraps of metal, and then re-formed, scraps and all, into the wall of the pipe.

"'Wow,' said the gnome, realizing that it was these tiny machines that were actually building the pipeline. The men on the outside were, well, they thought they were doing something, but in truth they were just sort of along for the ride. It was these tiny machines that were doing the real work.

"Finally, one of the robots came up to him, flashing its light bulb eyes in a friendly sort of way. It opened a compartment in its belly, and produced a plate with cheese and crackers. Gnomes love cheese and crackers! And fact is, he was pretty hungry from walking. The little robot held the plate out to the gnome. He took a bite. It was delicious."

Our car started to slow, another flagger, the perfect moment to emphasize something else in the story – I was listening to it as much as anyone. The best stories, for me, are the ones that I see, because it means that my imagination is engaged. I don't think about them. I don't practice or recount them. In fact, when I try to retell a story it usually goes sour. I like to be influenced by my environment. I like to weave the trees and roadsides into my tales. When I do, when I really listen, it's as if the earth in that moment speaks through me. Stories just happen. I merely have to watch. The words I speak are mostly just a description of what I see, or perhaps what I might like to see. So, I was in that car watching the story just like everyone else. None of us saw the same thing, but we shared it all the same. It happened inside us. I was merely the one speaking.

"Well, after the gnome ate his cheese and crackers, he looked up and saw the robots standing idly around him. He looked down at the platter, which had only a few crumbs left and suddenly he felt bad. He had eaten them all. He looked up with a guilty face, but then he saw something. One of the robots waved her arm in a friendly way, as if to say, 'no, no…it's alright.' She walked over to the wall of the pipe (she was the walking sort of robot), and knocked three times, bink, donk, dink. Suddenly, a large door swung open like a cabinet. Behind it, there were even more robots, and they started handing out little bottles of oil through the door. The robots passed them around, uncorked 'em, and drank 'em down…glug, glug, glug.

"The first little robot wiped her mouth on her sleeve. 'Ahhh,' she said, quenched by that peculiarly delicious beverage. Then they all raised their bottles in a toast and shouted, 'hurrah!' for the little gnome. He smiled.

"Well, goodness. The little gnome felt all warm and fuzzy at this point. He had been so surprised to find all these little machines in the metal pipe, and now they had all been so friendly to him. Gosh. But as he looked at his new friends, he remembered that he still had to get to Taos and he began to wonder how he would get there.

"One of the robots, sensing his thoughts, ran to the side of the pipe, tapped twice — bong, bong — and opened another little door. A shelf popped out and on it were a tiny pair of roller skates. The robot picked them up and offered them to the gnome, then explained that the pipe was downhill in the direction of Taos and he could ride inside almost all the way.

"Wow, thought the gnome. These guys are so nice. He strapped the skates on, looked at his friends, and almost felt a little teary. He was sad to say goodbye. 'Ah, don't worry,' said one of the robots, 'we're always here. You come visit anytime.' And with that, the gnome said thank you and waved goodbye to everyone gathered. He knew he'd see them again. The robots stepped to the side, waved and cheered. Finally, someone gave him a little push.

"At first, the gnome just rolled away slowly. He had time to turn around and wave once or twice, but soon enough he started to roll really fast. Bink-blunk, he hit the end of the pipe, where there was a little bump from the welding, then continued down the next pipe. Bink-blunk, bink-blunk, he passed pipe after pipe. He had miles to go, but aside from the welds it was pretty smooth sailing. Occasionally, there were more robots, but as he sped close they transformed and merged into the walls of the pipe. Once or twice, he turned around and watched. Once he had passed, the robots clink-bonked and grew out of the pipe walls again, then continued to do whatever it was they had been doing. He waved. They waved. It was amazing."

Once again, the cars coming the opposite way zoomed past, the pilot car turned around, the flagger reversed his sign, and our car started moving.

"Well, it was a long trip down that pipe. The gnome was roller skating for hours, making occasional strides and pirouettes. Because he was going so fast, he was able to ride sideways on the pipe walls and even upside down. Finally, after a really long time, he started to see something up ahead. A light. A bright light. A bluish, greenish, white light. And it was coming fast.

"Well guess what? It was morning. The gnome had been in the pipe all night long and as he approached the end it was beginning to get light out. It was Monday, actually, and the workers were returning after the weekend. Some of them had picked up their shovels. Some had climbed into their tractors and cranes, while others got out their welders. Of course, all this was completely unnecessary because it was really the robots inside the pipe that were doing the work. But people need jobs, so...

"Well, just as the gnome was approaching the end of the pipe, one of the crane operators lifted it up so he could start fitting it to the next one. But by now, the gnome was going too fast. Faster than our car. He was zooming down that pipeline. Suddenly, he realized he had to stop. How was he going to stop? He was going too fast. The light was getting closer and closer. There was really nothing he could do. He hit the last weld, bink-blunk, tilted up, and rocketed towards the opening.

"Poomp! *The little gnome sailed right out the end of the pipe…and into the sky. For just a second, one of the workers thought he saw a tiny little man with roller skates rocket out the end of the pipe. He rubbed his eyes, blinked, then grabbed his cup of coffee. 'I must be tired,' he thought.*

"Meanwhile, the gnome was sailing higher and higher into the air. He was going so fast, in fact, that he made it all the way to the clouds. Finally, he started to slow. He looked out at the miles of pipeline below, the blue sky overhead, the river that ran next to the road, the cars, the workers, the machines. It was so beautiful. All through the night he had been traveling that pipeline, gaining speed. Now, he was blasting through the air like a little gnome cannonball.

"Well, that's where we have to leave him for a second, just hanging in the air like that, because the robots at the beginning of the pipe knew exactly what was going on all along. They were no dopes. They had formed a little committee, and three of them were elected to climb down out of the pipe and head to the river. There was a blue heron down there who had tried to make her nest in the pipe once. There was a big to-do, but suffice to say she made it down by the river instead. Meanwhile, she and the robots had become good friends, just like the gnome. Well, the robots told her about the gnome. Christmas, hatchets, Germans, wood-chopping, all that stuff, and she flew off to the north. Just as the gnome started tumbling back to the earth, he landed on a soft blanket of feathers. Blue herons. Those dudes rule.

"Well, I could tell you more, but it's enough to know that the gnome made it to Taos. He helped cut kindling for a family, but only when they weren't looking. And he did their dishes at night. He strapped sponges on his feet and ice-skated while scrubbing their floors. The cats didn't like it, but they couldn't catch him. That's the kind of thing they do, anyway. Probably at your house too, but that's the end of the story. For now."

There was a brief pause in the car. We had passed the construction by now and were cruising toward our destination. Farmer Ron's is a magical place, with raspberries, apples, and corn the color of rainbows. It wouldn't be long. Finally, the silence was broken. "That was the best story ever!" the girls shouted from the back. "Can you tell another one?"

I smiled, then said, "Nope, I'm just going to tell that one." Sitting back, I looked at the open road, the last of the brown leaves shaking in the cottonwoods, and smiled pleasantly as the girls wheedled me for more stories. They kept at it for a minute or two, but I stood my ground. Telling stories can be spontaneous, wild and free, but it takes creative juice. It was only a minute or two before they accepted my finality and began retelling the story amongst themselves, this time with new twists and turns. My friend and I breathed freely, content with their giggles. This is the storytelling loop. A reality transformed by story into a new reality.

31

Be Yourself

Some people are natural, confident storytellers. Others feel fear. Some tell wild, tension-filled epics. Others describe a walk through the grass. Still others look for laughter. There are a million ways to tell stories, as many as there are people on the earth, and even individual storytellers will vary widely in their telling.

When you tell a story, it's you that you are giving to your child – your focus, love and attention. It's true that a good story can lift you up and take you somewhere, but you want to be sure that what you bring is authentic. The goal is not a perfect story. The goal is connection. Being a good storyteller, therefore, is mostly about showing up and paying attention. It's about being exactly who you are, whether you're a famous rock star or a quiet librarian.

At school, we sometimes like to put parents or visitors on the spot by asking them to tell a story. You can tell almost instantly who is comfortable in their skin. Folks who are simply themselves do it best. They search for a minute, then tell a brief story, maybe about a ladybug, a snowflake, or something unusual that happened that day. The stories are rarely amazing, but the kids love it. They're interested in who people are. They notice when someone is present with them. It doesn't matter if the story is a little short or strange. It's real.

Contrast this with parents, often highly intelligent, who wrack their brains, bite their lips, then make excuses because they're not prepared. They don't believe they can tell a good story, so they tell nothing at all. We've all been there. It's perfectly understandable. As adults, we forgive and forget. But the message, from the children's point of view, rings loud and clear – I have nothing to share with you.

Parents who stumble at story time are usually guilty of the Great Story Fallacy: in order to be a great storyteller, I have to tell a great story. There's nothing wrong with a great story, of course, but the search often results in a snipe hunt. We think we have to tell the biggest and most engaging story of all time. Aware of such blockbuster hits as *Spiderman* and *The Little Mermaid*, we quickly grow intimidated. Our search takes us outside of ourselves as we try to catch (or memorize) that elusive snipe and give it to our kids. That's fine if it works for you, but if it causes you to doubt yourself then it's not working. Come back and tell a simple story.

Sharing your stories means you have to value them, even the simple ones. And valuing your stories means you have to value yourself. You have to believe that who you are, just exactly as you are, is worth sharing. For most of us, this is not an easy task, but it's an important message to model to our kids. The intimacy of storytelling can actually be a great place to let your guard down and be seen. Stories from this perspective will win awards.

Start by relaxing your body. Find a place and a posture that is comfortable. Close your eyes if it feels natural. At school, we frequently tell stories while lying on the ground and staring at the clouds. Have your child lie next to you, or nearby. See if you can notice your chest rising and falling with your breath. Become present to your surroundings, but not occupied by them.

When a child says, "Tell me a story!" she is not asking for a narrative. She is asking for your attention. When that is fully given, stories begin to flow almost effortlessly. In time, this cycle of comfort, intimacy and story will build your craft faster than any expert's advice. You will no longer see storytelling as merely the repetition of a narrative, but as the sharing of an experience.

In such circumstances, your child will likely have no hesitation to return to storyland, but more importantly – neither will you. If our stories are accompanied by interior feelings of frustration or pressure to "do it right," they will be recorded in our minds as negative experiences even if the story goes off well. Telling stories will start to feel like work. But if you come from a place that is truly who you are, without any pretension, your experiences will largely be pleasant and attractive. Your memories will be filled with ease and peace, perhaps joy and laughter, even pride, making it easy for you to return.

This is your first goal, even before you tell your first story – be yourself. You can't tell good stories if you're lying. This rule is so easy, and so hard, that it makes and breaks storytellers. It doesn't matter if you're a fairytale mother with golden braids or a bus driver in gray slacks. Tell *your* stories. Be real. Your kids will love you for it.

As we come into plainclothes honesty with ourselves and our children, we can begin to explore what truly brings us joy and creativity. A storyteller should begin to pay attention to her schedules and moods. When do stories flow most easily? When do they feel like hard work? It's okay to say no when we're tired.

Part of the excitement of storytelling is watching a storyteller who is captivated with his own story. It grabs our attention. We mirror his enthusiasm. We see it in his facial expressions, and feel it in the tone of his voice. As Abraham Maslow and subsequent psychologists have pointed out, the expression of creativity is essential to a person's overall sense of well-being. A good storyteller, therefore, is enriched by his own process. He tells stories because he likes to tell stories, and he values the intimacy and connection they bring.

Practice #2 – Tell a Story to Yourself

Whether you have told children's stories before or not, take an opportunity now to tell one to yourself. Treat it just as you would a story with your child. Choose a time and location that is comfortable, and where there will be no interruptions. Look for an object or activity that catches your attention – whether immediately in front of you, or something from earlier in the day – and use it as a bridge into your story. Pay attention if you encounter laughter, curiosity, excitement, or perhaps uncertainty, discomfort or boredom. Is there anything you can do to make it more enjoyable? In the following hours or days, notice if you have any lingering connection with your bridge. Try repeating this practice in the morning, midday, and in the evening. Do you notice any differences?

Practice #3 – Tell a Story to Your Child

Perhaps you have already begun telling stories to your child. Or perhaps your child is not yet born! No matter the situation, take the opportunity to tell your child a story using the method outlined in the previous chapter. Choose a time and location that is comfortable, and where there will be no interruptions. Look for an object or activity that you know your child will recognize and use it as a bridge into your story. Pay attention if you encounter laughter, curiosity, excitement, or any uncertainty, discomfort or boredom. No matter what happens, let it pass. Don't hold onto it. Just notice it, and let go. Afterward, see if your child has any lingering connection with the bridge.

Sample Story – A German Village

By Silke Rose West

Raised in the desert of the American Southwest, I knew my girls would have a very different upbringing from mine in a small farming village in rural Germany. One of the ways I kept our family culture alive was by telling stories like the one that follows. I became the main character, the little girl. The stories were simple. As I told them, I tapped into many sweet memories that warmed my heart. My family was far away, my grandmother had passed on, but the stories kept us connected. That is the gift of a good story – it delights the teller as much as the listener. My daughters are now adults, but stories like these still captivate the children in my kindergarten. "Tell us about your village," they ask. What they mean is, "tell us about you."

Once, there was a little girl born in a village in Germany. Her parents were very busy with the cows and fields, so she spent much of her time with her grandparents, Oma and Opa, who loved her very much. Every Friday, Oma baked bread for Sunday, a special treat. The little girl looked forward to this bread, which was sweet and delicious, and so did the whole family. But one day, Oma did not have enough butter in the house to make the special bread. "What will I do?" she asked.

The little girl knew her grandmother would have to bake the bread, so she offered to go to the store. She was still young and could not yet read or write, but she was old enough to walk through the small village to the store. Everyone in the village knew her. She loved to talk and sing and hum, and would always greet the elders on the way. Oma had written a note: 1 pound of butter. *She placed it in a cloth bag along with a wallet that had money to pay for it. "Remember to hurry home after you buy the butter," Oma said, "Don't linger to long." Oma knew how much the little one liked to talk, and she had to get the bread in the oven before the church bell rang noon.*

On the way to the store, the little girl met the cuckoo-clock maker. The old man loved to show off his finished clocks, which were carved like great art pieces. He waved from his barn door to the little girl, and said, "Come see the newest clock! I just finished!" The girl stopped for a second, then said, "I must run to the store first, but I'll stop on the way home!"

The village shop had a special bell that rang to tell the shopkeeper that a customer had arrived. After all, it was her house and she had two children to care for besides the business. On that day, no one else was in the store and the little girl was helped immediately. "So, it is baking day and your grandmother ran out of butter?" the shopkeeper asked. "Yes," the girl replied, "and the money is in the bag too." She smiled. She felt very grown up. The shopkeeper, who knew the girl's family very well, put the butter in the bag with a receipt and the change. "Here is a gummy worm for you," she said. "Tell your grandmother that the new cloth will arrive next week."

The little girl loved running errands. She always got a treat and felt very proud that she could do her own shopping, though she was only five years old.

The cuckoo-clock maker was still waiting outside the barn door. "Look," he said, "here it is!" He had brought the clock outside, and the girl gazed at the beautiful handwork. "You are so talented!" she said. The old man beamed. "Now, I must hurry to grandma. I'll tell her about the new clock!" The girl waved and ran down the lane. The old man smiled. He was fond of the children that would take the time to admire his work. Most adults were too busy.

Grandmother had the fire going, everything was ready. She quickly took the butter and folded it in to the flour, milk, eggs and yeast. Her hands worked with such ease. Even though she was wearing an old dirty apron, she looked like a royal queen to the little girl.

Sunday's bread was so-o-o-o good. Every other day of the week, the bread was heavy and dark, but Sunday's loaf was light, soft and sweet. The little girl liked Sundays, after all that was the day she was born.

Start Simple
Start Young

The ideal time to begin telling stories is by the age of three or four. There is good reason to begin earlier, but if you haven't there will not be a lot of catch up required. By the age of five, a child often has a harder time adjusting to what feels like a sudden change and a new rhythm. This will be amplified if the child is accustomed to highly stimulating stories through movies, etc. The best time to begin telling stories is the first day of your child's life (or even in the womb), but at the age of three or four most children are still bonded closely enough with their parents that they will readily fall into the intimacy of story time even if it's a new experience. But there is a better reason to begin telling stories at an early age – you.

Storytelling, in the way that we're approaching it in this book, is about the relationship between you and your child. As a beginning storyteller, you will find it easier to begin when your child is still satisfied with simple stories. The practice and intimacy that you create in these early years will flow into further complexity as your child ages. In other words, your storytelling craft will naturally mature as your child matures. Plus, since your child will have become accustomed to storytelling from an early age, along with all its intimacy and comforts, he will not have a hard time differentiating it from the kinds of stories he finds on TV, movies, etc. He will likely prefer it in many contexts. In any case, there won't be much need for comparison, because both child and adult will recognize and feel the differences.

Simple stories for an infant or toddler can be very brief. Peek-a-boo is the first connecting story that simply says: "I see you, I love you. I discovered you, and you are the most precious gift!" As a child grows and starts to discover her own body, the story grows with her. We use our hands to pretend a little man is walking up a hill (the child's arm), he looks for a bell (the ear), and a rattle (the nose). These discovery stories help the child feel joyful in her own body and connect to the caregiver through gentle touch. Repetition and short sentences are the key. Patty-cake is another classic example.

A child who has begun to crawl, stand and explore her world is ready for short stories about objects. There was a little stone, it hopped to the edge of the table, then – *bloop!* – it dropped into the water. Such stories, when accompanied by your hand movements, the movement of the stone, and the splash of the water, can be very engaging for both parent and child. She will often want to hear them repeated, and perform parts of the story herself.

Around the age of two, an element of risk can enter in, e.g. a little boy walked away from mother and came to a big tree. He looked behind and what did he see? Oh my, a bear! Quickly, he ran back home to mother. A child at this age is not yet ready for the complex dangers and plots of modern stories, so keep it simple.

In the third year of life, a child forms friendships and is ready to take tentative steps away from mother or father, and the story grows. Now, the child that went behind the tree finds a friend in the bear, and together they start on a little journey, over a bridge, up a mountain to lie in a sunny meadow. As the sun gets ready for bed, they quickly trail back down the mountain, back over the bridge and arrive safely at home. Over time, we add more complexity, more friends, more excitement. By staying regularly engaged in storytelling, the evolution is effortless. You will have no trouble taking cues from your child, and vice versa.

Approximately at the age of four, sometimes earlier, a child awakens to the complex characters and plot developments we typically associate with entertaining stories. He also becomes eager to take plotlines and characters into his increasingly sophisticated and self-directed play. These are the kinds of stories we emphasize in this book. When used well, they are one of the most potent parenting tools available – for soothing, entertaining, teaching, and more – because they draw strength from the cycle of intimacy we've been crafting for years.

Something unique happens at four years of age. Psychologists call it "theory of mind." The classic experiment involves a small puppet show in a lab. A young child is taken to a small table where a team member uses a puppet or doll to place a small treat under a box. "For later," she might say. The puppet then leaves the stage. Meanwhile, a second puppet shows up and removes the treat, puts the box back in place, and leaves the stage. All of this happens under the watchful eye of the child. Finally, the first puppet returns, but before opening the box, the team member asks the child, "What do you think the puppet expects to find?" Until the age of four, most children will answer, "nothing."

Theory of mind is a complicated way of saying "another person's point of view." Young children are not fully capable of distinguishing another person's point of view. They might understand that mother or father is different, but they are as yet not fully capable of intuiting what mother or father is thinking, or that it's different from their own view. In the example above, they cannot restrain themselves from ascribing knowledge to the first puppet that it doesn't have. This changes at around age four, when a child's developing brain comes into full possession of this uniquely human tool.

As adults, we take theory of mind for granted, so that we hardly recognize what it's like to not have it. We walk into a grocery store and instantly ascribe intentions to the clerk behind the register, the man holding an apple in the produce section, two women chatting in the aisle, the children rummaging beside them, and the elderly couple now making their way for the door. Some scientists argue that a handful of animals display a rudimentary form of theory of mind, but there is no doubt in the scientific community that humans possess it with a unique sophistication.

Interestingly, it is also around age four that secrets begin to take a unique hold in a child's mind. Most two- or three-year-olds will honestly promise to keep a secret, then instantly turn and tell their mother or father, usually with little sense that they have broken a taboo, often to the irritation of older siblings. Lies are also more common in a four-year-old than a three-year-old. All of these phenomena arise because of theory of mind, this uniquely human tool to estimate the intention, knowledge, or perspective of another human or animal. It makes stories come alive with enticing complexity.

Stories are one of the primary ways we exercise this cognitive tool. By following distinct characters, with distinct points of view, we train ourselves to see the real world through an increasingly wide variety of lenses. We elicit a meaning that transcends that of the protagonist (or ourselves). This is one of the reasons stories remain compelling to us as adults. We naturally seek increasingly rich plotlines and characters because it gives us perspective.

It's important to remember that age four is just a marker, as are all of the age recommendations in this chapter. Some children develop a little earlier, some a little later. Using age four as a milestone, however, helps us understand why establishing a storytelling routine by the age of three or four leads more easily to a long and successful storytelling career with your child. If you missed the early years, you won't have too much trouble catching up at age four. But a child of five or six is a sophisticated little animal that is harder to catch.

Near the sixth year of life, real danger can be introduced. This is the age of fairy tales, witches eating children, and monsters in the wood. Before this, it is usually too terrifying to battle the witch or the monster alone. Now, a child might be ready, along with a little help from a forest friend, perhaps a little mouse who gets fed along the way. Some children dive right into stories like this, but many fear the challenges that accompany their developing maturity. Stories can help a child trust that it will end well.

In summary, we suggest starting to tell stories as early as possible, even before a child begins to recognize words. This helps set the tone for your child, but more importantly for *you*. This way, your craft slowly develops alongside your child. In infancy, stories are centered around a child's own body. As she develops, stories move to simple objects within her grasp. Taking cues from our child, we slowly progress into stories about mother or father and child, then a child on her own or with a friend, till around the age of four she is ready for complex adventures with multiple characters and occasional risks. If we have followed this progression with her, we will be perfectly comfortable telling stories with increasing levels of sophistication. The intimacy we have generated along the way will make it well worth it, and our child will have no hesitation to rest in our arms and listen to a story even as she approaches adolescence.

Practice #4 — Wholeness

In this exercise, we ask you to explore the world through the eyes of a three-year-old who has yet to develop the multi-perspectival "theory of mind." In this story, the child sees everything as part of himself — his mother, his father, the river, the sun. The child feels the joy of a flower or the sadness of a rainstorm as if they were his own body. If your child is older, you might frame it as a story about this curious child who cannot differentiate between himself and the rest of the world. If your child is very young, you might tell it softly as she drifts off to sleep. In any case, try to open your mind to what it would be like to experience the world as a wholeness in your own being.

Sample Story – Little Bear's First Walk

By Silke Rose West

Little Bear stories are one of the most common ways for parents to initiate storytelling. It could just as easily be little fox or little squirrel, but centuries of storytelling reveal human nature's particular penchant for Little Bear. This story is intended for a two- or three-year-old.

Once, there was a Mama Bear. She lived in a cave near a big mountain. Papa Bear had been going to fish. It was springtime and a lot of fish swam down the river. Mama Bear was waiting to birth her little cub, and when she saw him, she was overjoyed and licked his fur until he was nice and dry. When Papa Bear returned, he saw the beautiful cub and gave Mama Bear a big hug and a huge fish. Mama Bear needed to eat a lot, so that she could feed her little one.

One day, Papa Bear was gone for a long time and the little cub had grown enough to know the way to the river. Off he went down the trail, but he had forgotten to tell Mama Bear where he was going. All of a sudden, Baby Bear realized that he was lost and started to cry. A butterfly came and sat on his nose and he cheered up very quickly. Above in the tree was an old owl, who was startled by the cries of the little bear.

"Whoo, whoo are you looking for?" said owl.

"I am looking for Papa Bear," said Little Bear, "but I can't find him, and I don't know how to get back home."

"Oh, you silly little bear," replied owl, "your Mama Bear knows right where you are."

Little Bear turned and there stood Mama Bear with a knowing look. She had followed Little Bear quietly without making any noise. Little Bear called out to her, "I just wanted to find Papa Bear!"

"I know, here he comes," said Mama.

Papa Bear walked up the trail from the river with a big trout in his mouth. They gave each other a big bear hug and shared the delicious fish. "Can I go with you next time?" asked Little Bear. "We'll see," said Papa Bear, "it takes a lot of patience."

"Maybe the three of us can go together," Mama Bear offered. Little Bear smiled. The butterfly flew around the happy family, and the owl hooted good night, even though it was the middle of the day.

The end.

Establishing
A Rhythm

Storytelling takes practice. It's not about doing it right. It's about doing it regularly, then adjusting to what works for you and your particular child. In this chapter, we address several different topics related to time.

First is establishing a daily, weekly, or periodic practice. Choose a schedule that is realistic. As a beginner, this will help you stay committed. As your craft develops, your rhythm will do eighty-percent of the work for you, because you and the children will show up at the familiar place and time prepared to listen. Bedtime is an obvious choice. At school, we tell stories after lunch. Working parents may find it easiest to tell a story Saturday or Sunday morning.

No matter the time, it is helpful to set a particular storytelling spot, maybe a tree, a couch, or a bed. It can also be good to have a series of actions, like brushing teeth and putting on pajamas. Most important of all is the use of a short phrase or song at the beginning (and end) of each story. There's a reason many children's stories start with

"Once upon a time..." It sets the stage. In time, a practiced storyteller can call her children to storyland as predictably as Pavlov could whet his dogs' appetites with a whistle. In this way, the routines we set are themselves the bridge we take into storyland.

The verbal cue or routine can be of particular importance in unfamiliar settings, i.e. airports, cars, or even traumatic and dangerous situations. A child's anxiety or fear sometimes needs redirection. Telling a story can be an excellent way to introduce the comfort and intimacy of home in difficult situations and take one's mind off the stressful event. A soothed child equals a soothed parent, and a good story can feel almost lifesaving in certain situations. If you've ever been anxious with your child after a nightmare, an injury, or a car accident, you might have a sense of this. Story has the ability to catch our attention and hold it in a safe place, so we don't endlessly recycle trauma. By using a regular verbal cue, we can help bring a child quickly into that memorable place of comfort, often more readily than simply beginning the story itself. How do we get there? Regular practice.

Here's how one teacher does it. She sings a very short song about a few sailors getting on a boat and setting sail. It's not more than twenty seconds, but it sets a lovely stage for the story as we, the listeners, picture the sailors getting into the boat and drifting into the open sea. The melody brings us there. Then the story begins. At the end, she repeats an old closing, "Snip, snap, snout, this tale's told out," an alternative to "happily ever after."

Silke has several introductory methods, but most commonly uses the classic, "Once upon a time…" She also has a very old-fashioned song with monkeys chewing tobacco and ducks going *quack-quack-quacko*, which is so perfectly politically incorrect as to catch everyone's attention. Joe, like many fathers, is a little more sarcastic. He often begins his stories with a simple phrase and a shrug, "Alright, I'll tell a story. But you can't like it. No smiling." Whatever you choose, find something that feels natural to you. There is a lot of room for variety. Simplicity is the rule. If you're consistent, you'll come to see that a three-word phrase, or even a brief melody or tone, can quickly set the stage. If you don't believe it, consider what the chirp or ringtone on your phone does to your state of mind in a matter of seconds.

Some parents sense that they don't have enough time to tell stories. Life is already full to the gills. We can't possibly add one more thing. All of us face these challenges, but once we recognize that storytelling is a tool that builds intimacy and inspires productive play, we may find that it is a time-saving strategy, not an add-on. We've seen this work, both at home and at school, so many times we can't emphasize it enough – storytelling builds intimacy, meaning harmony, freeing up a lot of time otherwise spent bargaining or managing difficult behaviors.

Transition times in particular are often stressful events in our days, like getting ready for school or coming home from work. At these times, parents often have much on their minds and the distracted attention we give our kids sometimes leads to irritation, misbehavior or outbursts. Telling a brief story in these moments can be a uniquely helpful way to bring the family together, and sometimes five minutes is all it takes. Greeting a child with just five full minutes of undistracted presence within a few moments of walking in the door after work can replace the 30-60 minutes it might otherwise take to connect. It can also help us drop in and relax. Afterwards, it's often very easy for a child to go about her own tasks, freeing parents to do theirs. Everyone feels seen, and the whole house breathes easier.

What about drop-off and pick-up times at school or playdates? Have you ever had a challenging time getting your child to the car? What if you had a special story that you only told once you two were safely buckled inside? It could be something only the two of you know about – a secret! – maybe an ongoing adventure, slowly narrated over several weeks two minutes at a time. Stories like this give a child something to look forward to, rather than seeing it as just an end to play time, and they replace toy or candy bribes with the real thing – intimacy and connection.

Story is a good bridge in these moments because it takes the interview-like focus away from questions like *What did you do at school/work today?* and turns the moment into a common sharing. Truth is, we often don't want to rehash what happened earlier. We want to create intimacy now. For many children and adults, it is not easy to have someone blast in the door and give us too much direct attention. We like it a little slower, a little gentler, a bit more sideways. Storytelling is like wrapping your greeting in a big soft balloon. If we have an established routine, previously stressful transition moments might become deeply restorative. It will not feel like another thing to do.

Practice #5 – Once Upon a Time

Pick a phrase, song, or routine to start your next story. Make sure it's easy and memorable. You might also experiment with times of day and locations. There is no perfect recipe, but try to give a little attention to the ways you start and end your stories. You might find that it helps bring you, not just your child, into a calm and receptive mental state. Pay attention to what works. Let go of what doesn't.

Practice #6 – The Big Bad

Next time a stressful situation arises in your household, try telling a story. It will take some guts. But before all hell breaks loose, wave your arms and get everyone's attention. Then, just start telling it. You don't even have to know where it goes. If you can remember, pull one or two bridges into your story that everyone recognizes, but it's okay if your story has nothing to do with the moment. Two or three minutes is all it takes for our lungs and hearts to calm down. The story doesn't resolve the conflict, it creates intimacy. Shared intimacy is a positive influence that can help everyone drop their agendas a bit, so we can come back and resolve conflict more easily. In these circumstances, really bad and clunky stories are sometimes particularly useful. They're so bad, it's laughable. Laughing, even if you don't want to be laughing, is restorative. If you have a toddler who is resorting to tantrums, try this. If you have a wife or husband who comes home with glazed eyes, try this. Stories provide a meeting ground, not a zone to scrutinize conflict.

Sample Story – The Turtle That Did Not Want to Carry Her Home

By Silke Rose West

"Teacher, I'm tired! I don't want to carry my backpack!" the four-year-old complained. He often does this on Monday when returning to school. We were on our way to Happy Canyon, but the going was hard that day for all the kids. The sky was dark and the air was cold, but I knew he just needed a little attention and would be able to do it. We stopped at a small evergreen tree surrounded by mud and snow.

"Well, sit down my children and listen," I said. "Have you ever heard the story of the turtle that did not want to carry her house on her back?" I myself had never heard it, yet I began to see the story unfold before my eyes. The children looked at me, a little curious, glad to be taking a rest.

"Once upon a time, there was a little turtle that walked behind mother turtle. The turtle was tired of being a turtle and having to carry her house on her back. 'Mother,' she said, 'I don't want to be a turtle. Why can't I be a deer or a skunk instead? Then, I would not have to carry such a heavy weight. I could just go into the forest and run free.'

"'Oh, my little one,' replied the dear mother turtle, 'in time you will understand. Would you like to go see something big and fierce and dangerous?'" The little boy who had complained about

his backpack loved to fight pretend monsters and be seen as a fierce and cunning warrior.

"'Oh yes,' replied the little turtle.

"'Well,' said mother, 'I can only take you there if you carry your house on your back.'

"'Alright,' agreed the little one and slowly she followed her mother to the place where bobcat roamed. The mother did not fear the bobcat. She had many encounters before and knew that her shell served as great protection.

"Surefooted and confident, she led the way, the little turtle hurrying behind her. Bobcat, in the meantime, was excited to eat some turtle meat and pounced on mother turtle as soon as he saw her. Quickly, she hid her head and legs inside her house and patiently waited. The little turtle followed the mother's lead, and although bobcat pounced on little turtle, and even tossed her into the air, little turtle was safe. Bobcat's tongue licked little turtle's nose, but no teeth could penetrate through the hard shell.

"'I am so glad I have my house on my back to protect me!' she said.

"Bobcat shouted, 'well, I don't even like turtle meat. I am going to hunt myself a deer or a skunk. They do not have such hard, stupid shells!'

"After a bit of silence, little turtle stuck her head out and said to mother turtle, 'I am so glad I have a house that protects me, even if I have to carry it!'

"'I know little one, me too!'"

This little story gave us a moment to rest and redirected our attention in a loving and compassionate way. The little boy was not singled out, yet felt understood. Afterward, we kept walking without any complaints. The griping, the walking, the backpack — these were the bridges to our story. Because the children were accustomed to stories in these situations, and others, by the time I finished saying, "Have you ever heard the story of…" I had everyone's attention, and without demanding it.

Animals can be wonderful helpers in these stories. They help a child keep a safe distance and not feel threatened. If the story link is too direct, e.g., "There once was a boy who did not want to carry his pack," then the child might feel put on the spot and will not listen freely. The ending of the story provides a happy outcome that helps the listener feel encouragement with the difficult task that had previously been an obstacle. This is the storytelling loop: a real situation that led to an imaginative story, which helped give new meaning and purpose to reality.

# Nuts and Bolts

This chapter introduces an array of classic tools for building successful stories. In order to leave you with a few useful takeaways, we have divided this chapter into four sections: A Big World Full of Small Things; Color, Shape, and Texture; Puppets and Props; Developing a Theme. Practice exercises are provided for each section, and a sample story at the end to tie it together.

A Big World Full of Small Things

One of the most successful storytelling techniques of all time is filling simple, mundane objects with tiny operators. We find this in such classic tales as *The Shoemaker and the Elves, Honey I Shrunk the Kids, Gulliver's Travels, Horton Hears a Who*, and countless more. Fairies, elves and trolls fill the pages of classic literature, and are experiencing a renaissance today. Together with the personification of small animals, little beings in a larger-than-life world account for an enormous wealth of children's literature. Use it to your advantage.

Not everyone, however, likes fairies. The emphasis of this section, as in this book, is to help draw a child's attention to a given object or event to discover the imagination and creativity within. One of the surest ways to do that is to tell a story about a little gnome who lives inside a stone – that stone – and then describe what it looks like inside. But we can just as easily tell a story about ants who wake up and go sledding in winter. Bacteria have been known to skateboard down the dimples of an orange, and the story of an RNA sequence gone hopelessly awry is not so different from *The Sorcerer's Apprentice*. If we are religious, we might find tiny angels (or demons) in all sorts of things.

Whatever the particular lens, by keeping the story within an object or place that is recognizable, the storytelling loop gives us a chance to direct a child's focus and learn more. A child fascinated by the workings of tiny men in a stone will not only be entertained by the story but will also come to discover many real things about that very real stone. A story about tiny water people who gather in the clouds, then fall down as rain, only to be evaporated and "elevatored" back up to the sky can be a more engaging way to teach a young child about the water cycle than a factual lesson. A talented storyteller can use this simple strategy to direct a child's attention and spark curiosity in almost anything.

Practice #7 – Find Something Small and Make it Big

In this exercise, we invite you to find a small to medium sized object. This will be the bridge in your story, so be sure to select something your child will recognize. The challenge is to describe what it looks like on the inside or at a strange change in scale, as described by the tiny people, fairies, insects, etc., who live there. An example might be a globe that, to a tiny bug, is actually the whole world. He might go sailing. It could be your TV, and what the video characters do inside when you turn it off. It could be a mouse in your cupboard, or a squirrel in a tree trunk.

Color, Shape and Texture

A story comes alive when it is full of colors, smells, sounds and textures. This section emphasizes the use of descriptive language to attract and retain our audience's attention.

In the conclusion to his book, *On the Origin of Stories*, evolutionary theorist Brian Boyd emphasizes the importance attention has played throughout human evolution. As social creatures, he says, we are competing for each other's attention in subtle and gross ways. Those who garner the greatest amount of attention tend to be socially dominant. But social dominance (in other words, respect) is more graceful than forceful, and we can use it to our advantage. The surprise, color, action, change of pace, and sudden shifts in a story turn out to be important ways not merely to attract a person's attention, but to retain it.

A written story becomes suspect when every other sentence begins with *suddenly*. Not so for oral storytelling. In order to craft engaging stories, we need to constantly renew our audience's attention. That means we need action and curious things to happen. In a world where parents are competing with the storytelling skills of movie directors and cartoon animators – our stories have to have pizazz. Fortunately, the imagination makes it easy to do.

When telling a story, you're allowing a child to wander through her own imagination. By giving her colors, tastes and textures, the story (and her imagination) becomes a richer, more engaging place to be. If your character steps into a river, take a moment to say whether it is cold or warm, but don't linger too long on extravagant descriptions. Change your pace. Consider the anticipatory excitement of your character getting his toes wet, then his knees, the back of his knees, his thighs and waist, the excruciating moment the water rises above his belly-button, then reaches his shoulders, neck, lips, nose, eyes, forehead... *Goodness, is it ever going to get there?* He's under!

By drawing moments out like this, or having things change suddenly, along with all the colors and sounds, we give a child an opportunity to immerse herself fully in her own imaginative world. If we've used the storytelling loop, we give her a further opportunity – to bring that excitement and imagination into the real world.

Practice #8 – Enter the Cave

Caves feature prominently in a lot of stories. They represent something dark and mysterious. Find a bridge in a character, an event, or a place. Take your character inside the cave, and let everything go black. Deep inside, near the end, is a tiny light. There may be some sound. Walk towards it. Suddenly, you find everything is illuminated. Describe in fantastic detail exactly what you see. If it's scary, make sure there's some resolution. If it's beautiful, take a moment to enjoy it. Regardless of what happens, have your character return to the light of day when he's done.

Puppets and Props

The subject of puppetry is worth its own book. Sadly, most puppeteering books are about how to make puppets, not how to tell stories with them. They are mostly for experts. This section is not designed to help you stage an elaborate puppet show. It is intended to help the novice find puppets in common objects already likely to be in your home.

A puppet can be as simple as a small doll, or even a toy car. Taken in hand, it can explore the contents of the windowsill or junk drawer through the lens of that character. By taking on the voice of the puppet, some people find storytelling easier (if this isn't you, then feel free to skip this section). A story can even be told by the puppet, which takes some of the pressure off the speaker. Even a carrot can be a puppet, perhaps knocking about on the picnic blanket in search of something good to eat. In keeping with the storytelling loop, the puppet itself becomes the link to the real world, giving the child a chance to take the character into his own hands once the story ends. A child who has just witnessed his favorite toy perusing the contents of the junk drawer may just run off with it to find out what's under the couch.

These kinds of "table puppets" usually arise from spontaneous moments, but they can be expanded to include more intentionality. For example, a couple of dolls can be set on a table with a few stones or objects to stand in for a pond, a tree, a house, etc. As you tell the story, the dolls act it out, perhaps walking to the pond where they meet a friendly duck. Once complete, the entire set-up can be handed over to your child, who will often enjoy repeating the story with new elements, and maybe new characters. In this way, we're actively using toys, puppets and props as anchors in our story. When we hand them over to our child, we're giving them something more than a collection of toys. We're giving them an imaginative story that helps them engage. If you have a child that is complaining of boredom, or struggling to find something to do, this kind of story can be very helpful.

Another puppet that is easy for beginners to use is a sock puppet. All you need to do is put an old sock on your hand and draw two eyes. You can start by making simple *ahhh* and *ohhh* sounds that accompany the open and closed mouth of the puppet. This alone will make almost anyone laugh, including adults. Then, when you're ready, it can begin to speak.

Young children are fascinated by puppets, because they don't waste time doubting their reality. They make an immediate connection with this "third person," while you, the storyteller, begin to disappear. This is the secret for a good puppeteer – *make yourself disappear* – and it's what makes puppets, especially simple puppets, so helpful to the beginning storyteller. Puppets take the focus, relieving the pressure on the speaker and allowing those of us who might be a little shy to stay in the storytelling realm.

Imagine a puppet as a playmate that has come over to play with your child, or a grandmother that has come to visit from far away. It could be one of any variety of characters. Perhaps it is a dog puppet and stands in for the dog your child has often wished for. "Woof, woof," says the dog, "I feel like an old sock." The children giggle. "I wish I had some ears and a tail." *Hmmm,* we might say to the child, now in our own voice, *perhaps we can make it some!* Then, the dog leads us on a hunt for scrap cloth, and we sew two ears above the eyes. "Woof, woof," says the dog, "I feel so much better! Now, how about a tongue?"

With puppets, it can be a good idea to pause between storytelling. A child will naturally become an active participant and reply to questions, such as, "Do you have a dog?" If the child answers no, the dog can say, "I wish I had a child that would walk with me every day and teach me tricks, like jumping through a hula hoop! Then, I would go with my child to the circus and – woof! – we would make everybody laugh and clap hands. That would be fun!" The story can be directed by your child, who will naturally enter into a dialogue with the puppet. This also makes it easy for a parent or storyteller, who simply has to respond to a child's cues.

A storyteller also has the opportunity to use a puppet as a mediator in difficult situations. Let's stay with the dog puppet for a moment, and imagine a child that is afraid of dogs. "Hello," the dog might say, "my name is Spotty the Dog. What is your name? I am a nice dog, but I am a bit scared of children. Are you nice? Will you promise not to pull my tail? Oops, I don't even have a tail! I like to play catch, how about you? Would you like to hear my story about the child who pulled my tail and how I lost it?" This gives a child a chance to express himself and work out some of his issues in a safe setting. This sort of mediator can be very helpful when a child is angry with a parent or doesn't want to listen. Just send in Spotty.

When a story has ended, it can be a good idea to let the puppet say, "I have to leave now, but I promise I will come back." With the table-puppets described at the beginning of this section, we suggested handing the doll or set-up over to the child for further play. That works well for that kind of puppet, but the magical disappearance of a hand puppet can give it more character over time. This way, it will not just become another toy, but a character and a storyteller assistant. The key here is that the puppet is in your possession, not your child's.

Imagine the next day your child has a hard time getting ready for school. We might ask him to get ready, "because Spotty is waiting in the car, and he would like to sit with you on the way to school. Perhaps he can tell a story while I drive?" When you finally make it to the car, Spotty knows about your morning. He was a little worried that you weren't coming today. He was waiting for you. When your child says goodbye at school, to you and Spotty, he has something to look forward to at pickup time.

If your child loves to play with the puppet, you can offer to make one for him. Then, each of you can have a puppet, and the puppets can tell stories to each other or go on adventures. You can also make a simple puppet show theater out of a box and put on puppet shows for each other. A little song to start the show, perhaps a ticket for the audience... You can even start a puppet collection and do shows with different characters. Hand puppets are available at most toy stores, but we suggest that you don't buy them with your child. They are best introduced as a character by you. This keeps the storytelling magic alive. And remember, the puppets that depart or hide away in a special place will be more potent. If they simply become a part of your child's toy collection, they will tend to lose value. Why? Because the puppet is a tool for *your* storytelling.

Silke is a doll maker. She has a suitcase stuffed with dragons, kings, grandmothers, policemen, boys, girls, squids, birds and a menagerie of other characters made of wood, cloth, felt, wire, acorns, wool, knitting, and much more. This is her puppet suitcase, and it has traveled the world. The kids recognize the suitcase itself, and whenever it comes out, it has a special presence all its own. The beginning storyteller is not likely to take puppeteering to this level, but we hope that this section gives you a few ideas that you can use right now. If you're interested in a deeper exploration, there are a variety of books available specifically on puppetry.

Silk or cloth marionettes are another easy puppet to make and have a wonderful angelic quality. They are particularly lovely at bed time if you turn off the light and light a candle. The marionette can sing a bedtime song and tell a simple story that helps your child calm down and go happily to sleep. Perhaps the puppet comes to collect any worries of the day and tells the dream fairies that it's time to come. These marionettes are easy to make out of a square piece of silk or cloth. Fold it diagonally into a triangle, and create a head at the center of the fold with a pinch of stuffing and tie it off. Then, make a smaller knot on each outer corner for the hands. Three strings attached to the head and two arms is all you need to move this puppet with magical realism.

We'll end this section with one last puppet idea. Randolph is a hand-knit doll about the size of this book. In hand, he laughs to the kids while looking at the hole in his foot. "Ah, my maker was a bit sloppy with her stitches when she made me, but I don't care!" he says. "I'm not worried about getting torn or dirty. And look, I found some paint brushes!" He's a bit mischievous. Randolph picks up a brush in his hand, picks his favorite color, and dances with the paintbrush on the paper. "It's like sweeping with a broom!" he says. Randolph is delighted. The kids are delighted. Painting becomes a story.

Practice #9 – Change Your Voice

This exercise requires a bit of courage. Find a doll or a figure – anything, it could be an apple – that somehow connotes to you a personality distinct from your own. Then, have the figure tell a story to your child. If you're a fairly happy person, you might find a soggy, unhappy banana who isn't excited about anything. If you're temperate, maybe you find a race car that's a little risky. Whatever it is, allow the character to take away some of the pressure you might normally feel. It's not your story. It's the character's story.

Developing a Theme

A practiced storyteller usually has one or more themes to draw upon, whether a repeat character that has already navigated several adventures in the past, a setting like a castle and village, or an approximate set of rules for fairies and gnomes that one takes for granted in certain whimsical circumstances. By stepping directly into one of these themes, we sometimes take a shortcut into storyland. We might also develop a richness or subtlety otherwise difficult to achieve in one telling. At the same time, an overused theme tends to get rusty. It's good practice to mix it up.

Most commonly, a storyteller develops a theme from one particularly good story. It's usually easy to take those same characters on a new journey, and after a few tellings we usually have a primary setting and the basic "rules" of the story. In this way, we create a theme almost without thinking about it. Themes, however, usually represent deep-seated values, as illustrated in the following example.

When the two of us began telling stories together, we discovered a funny hiccup. Silke loved to tell stories about kings and queens, princes and princesses. She had an entire medieval village stocked with bakers, millers, dragons and wizards, and she trotted these characters out regularly. Joe, a bit of an urban skeptic, had a hard time swallowing it. For him, the theme was jaded and reeked of hierarchy and sexism. So began a long and interesting process, a conversation within stories, that teased out some of our values and assumptions.

It was regular practice for us to share stories with the kids after lunch. Silke often began the tale, then passed the story to Joe to finish. We had a lot of common values, but our storytelling methods could hardly have been more different. The stories that resulted were a strange hybrid, some of which soared like magic. Others fell dead like giants. Beneath it all, a dialogue never entirely visible to either one of us spoke of the themes, or values, upon which our own lives were built.

For Silke, who literally grew up in a small German village only miles from a medieval castle, the village was a meaningful allegory for the entire person. Each character played an archetype. The king and queen weren't tyrants, they were tasked with the oversight and governance of the entire being. The dragon wasn't evil, he was necessary, mysterious and dark. The baker thought of food, and the farmer planted whether there was war or drought. Princesses didn't just wear frilly dresses, they pierced the truth with their eyes like knights pierced armor with lances. And just as all these archetypes had their roles, so too did their failings and deviations.

Joe's initial reaction had much to do with individual sovereignty, a common theme in the urban American landscape into which he was born. Time and again, his princesses and millers sought freedom and self-expression, sometimes at the expense of isolation. In the end, we learned a tremendous amount from each other, and our stories grew. All of it, largely unspoken. The children, of course, were never directly conscious of this process, but they did witness the stories' evolution throughout the year. In so doing, they too explored these themes and values for themselves.

Practice #10 – Open the Pantry

It is often easier for a storyteller to develop one or two protagonists. In this exercise, we ask you to visit your pantry and let each can of beans speak for itself. Imagine the arguments between spaghetti and rigatoni. Does anybody get stuck in the putter butter? What does the oatmeal have to say? Is there a chocolate bar? Try to explore how this simple setting could be the springboard for multiple volleys into storyland.

Sample Story - Squirrel Naughty Foot

By Silke Rose West

The story below unfolded over a whole year after it was first told spontaneously to children waiting for the car pool. Two students of mine, siblings, sat in the back of my car. Boredom had led to a teasing game which ended up with the girl kicking her brother. She had no intention to stop even when I asked her repeatedly. I decided to redirect with a story.

"Have you heard of Squirrel Naughty Foot?" I asked.

"No, please tell us!"

"Well, his name was not always Naughty Foot. He had a beautiful name given by his mother. But when he was young, he liked to kick any animal that came near him and he even thought it was funny. Now, the other animals, you can imagine, did not like it. Some snarled at him. Others hissed and eventually they all avoided him, and said, 'There comes Naughty Foot, quick run away!' So, it was the animals that spoke his name so often that caused his real one to be forgotten. It didn't take long for Naughty Foot to feel lonely, and even he had forgotten his own name."

This part of the story taps into the situation that took place between the children and helped them to feel seen, and yet not judged. The story character takes the pressure off the child and leads to an anticipation of what will unfold. We arrive at the place where we are stuck and need a solution.

"'What is my name, mother?' he asked. The wise squirrel mom told him to go and find out for himself. She gave him a sack of nuts and sent him off. Squirrel Naughty Foot came to Raccoon and asked, 'What is my name?'

"'Naughty Foot, what else?!' said Raccoon.

"Thereafter, the squirrel came to Bear's cave and asked the same question, but the bear only replied, 'Your name is spoken throughout the forest and surely you know what it is.'

"Now, Naughty Foot scurried through an oak grove. As he did, he stumbled over a tree root. He hurt his foot and sat down and started crying. From behind an old oak came a gnome. He tapped on the squirrel's tail and said, 'Hello Scamper!'

"'I am not Scamper, my name is Naughty Foot!'

"'Oh well,' said the gnome, 'it seems you have come to love the name the animals gave you. Perhaps you should keep it but learn to do helpful things with your feet and then you won't be so lonely. Why don't you take your bag of nuts and put one in front of each animal den? The animals will see your foot prints and know it was you. But don't wait for them to thank you. If you do this three days in a row you will see that something magical will happen.'"

We are at the part of the story where the children get excited and want to know what the outcome will be. You can choose your own ending; in my case, it leads toward the shift that I would like to see the children make in their behavior with each other.

"On the way home, Naughty Foot scurried and distributed the nuts throughout the forest in front of the animal dens. When he got home, he asked his mother for more nuts. 'My name is Naughty Foot,' he said. 'That is the name I want to keep. I like having a funny name! I know that it used to be Scamper, but that will become my secret name.' The mother saw how happy Naughty Foot was and nodded wisely.

"Over the next two days, Naughty Foot distributed nuts throughout the forest and the animals started to whisper about Naughty Foot and decided to give him a chance to play. They had a game called 'Kick the Pine Cone' and Naughty foot was very good at it and they all praised him. He turned to his animal friends and said, 'Thank you for my name! I will use my feet wisely from now on, but I want you to call me Naughty Foot.' And this is how Naughty Foot got his name."

The two children that had listened to the story had big smiles on their faces. The story gives you a chance to share your values with children and guide them gently towards right action. It requires the storyteller to look for the good, and trust that this is enough. There is no interpretation needed thereafter.

The next day, the children asked, "Can you tell another Naughty Foot story?" I told the story of how Naughty Foot helped his friend Skunk. In that story, Naughty Foot became the hero that was a helper to other creatures. The stories carried on throughout the year during car pool times. Sometimes a child would ask me to tell a Naughty Foot story to a friend who had lost his or her kindness. The children understood how helpful a simple story could be. For me, it is one of the greatest teaching tools.

# Stories to Soothe

One of the principal features of storytelling is its ability to capture and redirect a child's attention (or an adult's). In chapter one, we called this the storytelling loop. If we start with a normal set of circumstances, then introduce a story, we usually return to the same set of circumstances with a new perspective. For the beginning storyteller, this usually means whimsical stories intended to entertain and foster creative outlets for play. Stories like that will likely remain the bedrock of every storyteller's practice, but as your craft develops you will begin to see storytelling opportunities in a variety of circumstances.

Put simply, narrative structure is a powerful tool for gaining attention. If you have ever struggled to gain a child's attention – and who hasn't? – you might consider telling a story. It often mitigates the conflict and frustration associated with direct inquiries or demands. Plus, once gained, a skilled storyteller can redirect that attention towards any object or activity she chooses. This is the essence of the storytelling loop. In the following chapter, we're going to talk about how this can be a potent teaching tool, but in this chapter we focus on the therapeutic effect of stories.

Stories are inherently soothing. No matter the subject, they give an ailing child attention, and they do so without drawing her focus onto the problem. Children who have been injured, ill, or suffered some emotional trauma can become fixated on the problem. We see this in behaviors as diverse as a two-year-old's tantrum and a preteen's despondency. Both can be greatly aided by story. The emotional intimacy helps them to feel connected, calm, and sometimes a little stronger.

A student of ours once knelt down unwittingly onto a cactus. It was a cholla cactus, one of the nastiest in New Mexico because its inch-long needles have barbs at the end like a fishing hook. It hurts going in, but it's much worse coming out. We occasionally have to deal with one or two needles, but this particular time the child had landed on a six-inch long section that now clung to his shin like a giant thorny lizard. As the initial bites of pain rolled into his consciousness, this boy, five years old, began to freeze. He knew what he had gotten himself into. His teeth clenched and he stopped breathing altogether. The pain was real, but the thought of what was to come was almost unbearable.

Joe slowly eased toward the child, calmly repeating, "breathe, breathe…" Meanwhile, Silke, having surmised the situation, called some friends over. "Josh, Tim, help your friend Michael out by telling a funny story," she said. Josh and Tim took one look and immediately recognized the severity of the situation. They immediately fell into the most hilarious antics, recounting the best events from the week, waving, shouting and playing the goof. Michael's face, clenched in a painful expression, began laughing, then clenching, laughing and clenching. You could hear the struggle in his voice. Finally, as the stories got the best of him, Joe slowly reached for the cactus. With one quick yank, Michael's pant leg went taught and the cactus came out. Michael's face went bright red, then he stood up, doubled over, and finally waved us off. "I'm alright," he said, fighting back tears, "I'm alright." Five minutes later, after a quick checkup, he was back playing with his friends.

There are times in life when there's nothing to do but face the pain. If we take it head on, however, we sometimes multiply the trauma by giving every excruciating ounce of our attention to our despair. Focusing on solutions or alternatives sometimes only feeds the flames because it keeps our energy focused on the problem. In these moments, stories can be unique medicine. If, as recommended in Establishing a Rhythm, we have a verbal cue or routine that introduces story time, we can sometimes use it in difficult circumstances to reach into a child's consciousness and flick the switch towards safety and intimacy faster than aspirin or ibuprofen might hit their bloodstream.

It might strike some readers as bombastic to claim that storytelling can be this effective. Mostly, we think of storytelling as a sort of entertainment. But if we grasp the intimacy at the core of the storytelling relationship, along with the evolutionary arc of the human organism to grasp information and meaning through narrative structure, we begin to see how this uniquely human tool can help us dial in and connect with our kids in rapid and effective ways. Equally as important, the intimacy of storytelling is a two-way street: a soothed child is a soothed parent.

A mother was getting the cake ready. The birthday girl was excitedly passing out party favors, the kind that roll out when you blow into them, then zip back up when you stop. *Zip! Pfffft! Wree!* All the kids were having fun until the birthday girl realized she had passed out all the favors and none were left for her. As her friends buzzed around, blowing raspberries and giggling, she began to cry. Her mother, lighting the candles, suddenly took notice and felt uncertain. Kids, mother, parents, birthday child – everyone was feeling something different. Chaos nearly ensued, but then someone shouted, "Hey, have I ever told you about…"

Stories take the pressure off. They grab attention, and then redirect it to something useful. They help synchronize the emotions of speaker, listener, and everyone gathered. It does not need to be a twenty-minute thriller. A one-minute episode is often all it takes.

Practice #11 – Soothe the Pain

The next time a difficult situation arises for your child, try telling a soothing story. It might be a physical pain, or a difficult emotion. It might be a nightmare, or even a moment of conflict between the two of you. Whatever it is, make sure it's not something that can be easily fixed by some other method. The goal is not to use story as an excuse, it is to witness how story is sometimes the only medicine available.

Sample Story - Ramona & Peter

By Joseph Sarosy

"Owie! Daddy!" my daughter yelled. It was the middle of the night and I could hear the anxiety in her voice. I so desperately wanted to sleep, but instead I shook myself awake and stood up. There was no ignoring it. We had been through this many times before. "Hey, pup," I said, easing myself down next to her. I snuggled close. As I did, I felt her whole body squirm. She was so angry.

A rash my daughter had developed a year ago had suddenly come back with a vengeance. During the day, when life was good and distractions were many, it was almost negligible, but at night, with a silent room in total darkness, the itch was torturous. We had been to the doctor. We had given her the medications. None of it worked, a fact we knew from the previous outbreak. It was simply a matter of time. As parents, it was excruciating. The lack of sleep was getting to all of us, but mostly it was having to look our daughter straight in the face and admit that there was nothing we could do.

Except, there was. After lightly washing the rash in cool water and reapplying the topical cream, I lay down next to her in bed. "I'm going to tell you a story," I said. "But, remember that one from the other day, with the sea turtles and all that?"

"Yeah."

"This one isn't as good."

Humor. It's my way in. She shook her head, but I could already feel the relaxation flowing into her muscles. I had begun to suspect the rash was related to stress, a stress my six year old daughter did not yet have language for. "It's about Ramona," I said, conjuring up the name from somewhere, probably The Ramones. "Have you ever seen the turkey vultures down by the gorge, circling and soaring?"

"Yeah."

"Well, Ramona was a turkey vulture. She loved to spread her wings wide and pick up the warm drafts of air that rise off the mesa. She was magnificent, really. Just beautiful, a long-feathered bird soaring on the wind." I couldn't see my daughter's face, but I knew that she was smiling. We've shared countless hours telling stories together, so she knew how to drop right in. I didn't know what the story was about. I had just picked a bird, a bird she would recognize from hundreds of sightings, and I had made it a female so she could identify with it.

"Well, Ramona was out flying because she was looking for a place to build a nest. She had only recently left her parents. She had been sleeping at night in branches and cliffs, but she knew in her heart that it was time to find a place of her own. Just as she was flying past Bone Canyon [a local landmark I knew my daughter would picture], she saw the perfect place. It was right in the middle of a steep cliff, a little ledge just wide enough for a vulture, nothing but vertical rock above and below. The bobcat would never be able to reach her there.

"Now see, the bobcat — he was often nearby, lurking behind the sage and pinons. A vulture was never an easy catch — I mean, they can fly — but if one roosted too near the flatlands, the bobcat would sometimes sneak...slowly...up...and snatch 'em!" I paused for effect.

"No, daddy," my daughter said, "I don't like scary stories."

"I know," I answered, "but I'm telling you, this spot Ramona had was incredible. There was no way the bobcat could get to it. Nobody, except a vulture. Or, you know, a swallow or canyon wren, but they mostly kept to themselves. Anyway, Ramona checked it out. From the ledge, she could look down at the Rio Grande below. She could see far to the north, and far to the south, and when she was ready, she opened her big wings...pwooh...and flew into the gorge.

"She spent the whole day gathering twigs and grass, and all sorts of things for her nest. And when she was done, pfft, you know what?"

"What?"

"She was hungry. Well, and what do vultures eat? You know. I know. Ain't no reason to fool around. They eat dead animals. That's what they do. They don't hunt down and kill stuff. They just fly around and look for stuff that's already dead. Pfft! I don't do that. You know how they do it?"

"Huh?"

"Sniff-sniff…they smell for it." I made a few audible sniffs, in her ear, like an overeager dog. "I mean, they look too. They're good lookers, just like eagles, but they have particularly good sniffers and they just love the smell of rotting meat. Isn't that funny? Can't blame 'em. Just how it is."

"Gross."

By this point, my daughter hadn't scratched for several minutes. She was fully relaxed. She had her father by her side, and all her attention was wrapped up in the story. I had made a point of varying the sensations, the audible whiffs, the sights and sounds. This came easily by just picturing the scene and then describing what I saw. I wasn't searching for narrative structure, or plot. Instead, I kept my audience engaged by varying the language and cadence of my delivery. All of this was a bit of a charade, but the underlying message was I'm relaxed enough to be an idiot. My daughter, hearing that message through the familiarity of her father's goofy mannerisms, echoed that relaxation in her own body.

What is storytelling? In this particular circumstance, if I said it was about a turkey vulture named Ramona, I think I'd be missing the point. The communication that happened between my daughter and me had almost nothing to do with the content of the story. It had to do with the context of the night, the previous nights, even the previous year, and a father's attempt to soothe his ailing child. There were words, no question, but the core communication

89

was unspoken and invisible. If you grasp this essential point, everything else in the book is secondary. You're not looking for a good story. You're looking for a good relationship.

Dr. Gordon Neufeld calls it attachment. In his book Hold Onto Your Kids, he emphasizes how a strong bond of attachment is the foundation of a healthy child. Dozens of scientific studies point out how storytelling develops empathy in children. It helps them broaden their experience of the world, increases emotional literacy, builds resilience, and so on. Almost all of this research, however, is focused on the relationship of the child to the story itself. In other words, it's the narrative most scientists are studying. It's relevant, to be sure, but Dr. Neufeld's attachment theory helps fill a gap in storytelling science. It explains the intimacy we find at the heart of the storytelling relationship. Storytelling, as we're learning, isn't merely about the plot, it's an effective tool to build attachment between any two people, including parent and child, and healthy attachment leads to a royal flush of desirable traits.

Ramona eventually found a dead skunk at the edge of the gorge. It was deliciously rotten and stinky, and she had it all to herself. As she was eating, the bobcat took notice and slinked up behind her. Slowly, he approached, Ramona blissfully unaware in a stench of rotting meat and skunk glands. The sad truth is that the bobcat almost got her, would have gotten her, if it had not been for another vulture, Peter, soaring high above, who saw the bobcat and came swooping in at the last minute. It was just long enough to distract the bobcat, and for Ramona to fly safely into the canyon below.

Turkey vultures falling in love. We've all been there. I'll spare you the rest of the story, which ends with my daughter falling asleep as first one, then two eggs are laid. She slept the rest of the night. Me too. The next day, her mother and I had a conversation with her about something that might have been bothering her more than we realized. As we helped our daughter give language to that stressor, she felt relieved. Within a week, the rash had all but gone away. There was not even one more sleepless night.

Maybe it was the medicine. Maybe it was her immune system kicking in. Who knows? The physical symptoms remain mysterious to me, but there's no question that Ramona and Peter were a big part of getting my daughter to sleep that night. What's more, it furthered our connection. It offered me, an uncertain parent, a way to connect with my daughter when I otherwise felt helpless. That's powerful stuff. My daughter and I spent a good number of hours in the following weeks fleshing out further details of Peter and Ramona's story, which eventually turned into the tales of Pal and Pam, their nestlings. The bobcat returned, then got hopelessly wet in the river. We all laughed. Eventually, we grew weary of the theme and let it go. The best part was walking by Bone Canyon a few weeks later. A swift wind brought two vultures into view as they rose out of the canyon and over our heads. "Ramona!" my daughter shouted. I smiled. "Peter!" I said.

# Stories to Teach

The intimacy we've created with regular story time allows us to slowly give birth to expanding layers of depth and meaning. In the last chapter, we talked about how stories can soothe an ailing child. In this chapter, we will look at how stories can help focus a child's attention in order to teach valuable lessons. Perhaps most importantly, stories help a child *retain* those lessons.

Narrative structure has a way of sticking in our minds. In study after study, compared to rote facts, it has been shown to increase a person's ability to remember material anywhere from 600 to 2,200 percent. In contrast, as psychologist Hermann Ebbinghaus famously (or infamously) demonstrated in "the forgetting curve," almost 70 percent of information is forgotten in one day. Ebbinghaus published his study in 1885 and his results have consistently been reproduced by scientists, helping to form the foundation of memory science. The essential point is this — memory has as much to do with how information comes in as how it comes out. Attention plays a key role, telling the brain where and when to lay down tracks for the incoming information. As we all know, however, attention is a limited resource.

Storytelling, along with its central characters, emotional gravity, unusual plot developments and descriptive language, is one of the most powerful tools we have for gaining and retaining attention. The result is a tight package of information laid down over multiple avenues into our memory banks, making it just a little easier for us to beat the forgetting curve.

It is usually easy for us to recognize this fact. We naturally give our attention to a good story, and wince at the thought of an afternoon lecture. Children are no different. If you engage their attention with a good story, they usually remember it. But attention is not the only factor at work in making storytelling such a powerful memory tool. Briefly summarized, we have three other factors: chronology, replay, and positionality.

Narrative has a chronological order. This allows us to find a detail (or fact) in the story quickly, because we are able to hone in on it by relating it to what came before or after. It has an inherent organization. Conversely, a loose collection of facts is much more difficult to recall, because it lacks an internal structure. Shawn Callahan, author of *Putting Stories to Work*, reports a study by A.C. Graesser at the University of California that gave students a collection of twelve readings, some narrative, like *Noah's Ark*, some expository, like an encyclopedia entry. The narrative texts were read twice as quickly, yet students retained twice as much information as they did from the expository texts.

Because stories are often entertaining, we naturally replay them in our heads just for fun. If important facts or lessons are strategically placed within the story, a person recalls that information every time they retell the story. This is the backbone of memory, and it's called neural plasticity. In his bestselling book *The Brain That Changes Itself*, Dr. Norman Doidge puts it this way, "Neurons that fire together, wire together." In other words, the more frequently neurons are fired, the more the connections are strengthened – making it more likely that we'll recall the information again. The opposite is true for neurons that rarely fire. In fairly short order, usually while you're sleeping, the brain simply wipes them out. Doidge calls this, "Use it or lose it."

Stories help us gain attention, they give us an inherent chronological order, and they encourage us to replay the story and solidify the neural content in our brains. Pretty high-tech, really. But they do one more thing for us that is worth touching upon: positionality.

Stories are uniquely effective at taking the pressure off the speaker and listener. Pointed information, even when lovingly well-intended and received, has a tendency to create a dichotomy, a me-versus-you or us-versus-them. *I am the teacher and you are the student,* or *I am the parent and you are the child.* Even in the best of circumstances, this positionality can create problems. On the other hand, a story isn't directed at anyone. It creates a useful fiction – third person narrative. It's just a story. The information provided, in context, allows a child the opportunity to feel as if she is discovering it for herself. To paraphrase Chapter 17 of the *Tao Te Tching:* When the master governs, the people hardly know he exists... When his work is finished, everyone says, "Wow, we did it all by ourselves!"

If you have ever had a battle with your child (or partner) over some little task, you will sense the gravity of positionality. Humans get bogged down in it, and the informational content goes out the window. Instead, we now have a power play on our hands. If you sense this might happen, try telling a story and include the information or value in the narrative.

So, this is how we teach. By telling stories. First, we grab a child's attention with an interesting character or plotline. If we've already established a storytelling routine, as suggested in Establishing a Rhythm, we know how to dial in quickly. By taking a recognizable object or activity into our story, as described in the storytelling loop, we immediately tie our child's attention into a real place in the very real world. Now, in the midst of our story, we redirect that attention to a subject that is pertinent, maybe the ABC's or a particular value we want them to have. We keep the story engaging by using descriptive language, changes of pace, and sudden events so that we don't lose our child's attention. Then, throughout the story, or maybe at just one or two key points, we plug memorable words, facts or lessons into the details of the story. This can be overt, as in the "moral of the story," but often it is incidental to the plot, for example a message written on a wall, or a big yawn and stretch by a growing cell that describes the process of mitosis. When we end the story, we close the loop, returning to the real world with a new lens to help our child comprehend *and retain* difficult material.

This might sound complicated, but it's outstandingly simple, because people have been doing it for 60,000 years. Here's an example. A group of children bickering over control of the "one" stick or the "one" doll can be told a story in the guise of a group of animals with similar problems. By allowing the characters to behave in both respectful and disrespectful ways, each child has the chance to see how the actions affect others and the group as a whole. For young children, this is often much more effective at eliciting comprehension and fostering cooperation than reprimands or directives, which tend to isolate and divide (positionality), and lead to further defensive behaviors.

Storytelling also allows us to simulate activities, including emotions, that are sometimes too dangerous or heart-wrenching to practice in real life. This itself is a form of instruction, and we see it in many fairy tales and "scary" stories, as well as in modern movies and the tragedies of Shakespeare or ancient Greece. By exploring plot lines that would otherwise overwhelm us, we gain some perspective on difficult situations we might eventually encounter.

Academic lessons can also be greatly aided by story. When Joe was teaching his first-graders to read, he was looking for a mnemonic device to distinguish the vowels from the consonants. He ended up telling a story about two friends, Ayee and P-tip. The weird names grabbed the kids' attention right away. P-tip was a singer, a beat-boxer actually, who entertained his friends with elaborate, "*boom-tip, peh-peh, tip*," beats. It was rad, and the funny sounds pulled the kids in even deeper. But one day, as Ayee and P-tip were growing into adults, they ventured high up the mountain and encountered a dragon. They were almost killed, but at the last moment Ayee pulled P-tip to safety, but not before the dragon burned P-tip terribly with his breath of fire. P-tip almost died, but after a long convalescence he regained his strength. Sadly, he could no longer beatbox, because his lips were forever scarred. He was depressed. Ayee had moved away and was now living on another continent. Slowly, P-tip learned to sing again, this time with his throat, and he recorded a huge international hit. Ayee heard it for the first time on the radio. It went like this, "Ayee, I owe you…"

Such stories make the kids laugh, shout and sing. Afterward, they had no trouble recalling the letters A, E, I, O, U, even though the story had nothing much to do with them. Interestingly, much of what we've written about storytelling could be said for song and melody as well. Combining the power of the two creates a highly fertile memory bank in a child's mind from which he can not only extract future recollections, but upon which he can slowly attach and build new concepts. In Ayee's case, all it takes is the melody, "Ayee, I owe you…" and the kids are instantly tuned in to letter recognition and reading comprehension. They recall the story, the real lessons we learned in the classroom, and most importantly–the excitement and energy which is our entry point into the subject, not the deflation and sighing of, "okay kids, get out your workbooks."

Stories are also one of the primary ways we pass on cultural and religious values. Most of our religious texts are filled with stories. They are an intrinsic part of every holiday. All of it information, pouring into the ears and hearts of the newest generation. As parents and caregivers, we can replay those classic stories verbatim. We can also tap into those established storylines and tease out messages and values uniquely useful to our children at this time.

A child can also be greatly aided by a story before rites of passage (like losing a tooth) and difficult times (like a friend moving away). As parents, many of us have been trained to look for the right book or the right video in such situations. There's nothing wrong with that. We benefit from all kinds of stories. But if we've grasped the potency of the method described in this book, and we've invested the time to cultivate the intimacy and comfort of story time with our children, we may find oral storytelling is uniquely potent for helping a child make meaning of some of the biggest events in life. That might sound intimidating, but if we've started with little bear stories at age two, it won't feel like such a leap to create stories about becoming a woman at age fourteen.

Practice #12 – Embed a Message

Think of a simple message or lesson you might like your child to remember. It might be about putting toys away, not hitting, or the fact that every sentence ends with a period. Anything. Make it yours. Whatever it is, be sure the kernel can be contained in a simple message or phrase. Next, tell a story where the message shows up, perhaps written on the wall of a cave, or spoken by a wise and mysterious owl. Remember, it can be central to the plot, but also incidental.

Practice #13 – Embed a Context

A potent teaching tool is to present a particular value or lesson merely as the context or frame of the entire story. For example, a story about religious tolerance can be overtly about a Jewish boy celebrating Chanukah with his Christian friend, and vice versa. Such stories can be wonderful, but occasionally heavy -handed. Sometimes, even if the protagonists create understanding and reconciliation, the underlying message is that such an understanding is lacking in the culture at large. Alternatively, a story about a tolerant village where the candlemaker is busy making green and red candles for Christmas and blue and white candles for Chanukah, then some terrible mix-up or funny event happens, might send home the same message to your child – we celebrate diversity – but without making the conflict central. In the end, maybe everyone has rainbow-colored candles.

Sample Story - The Urangee Kanighit

By Joseph Sarosy

"Sire! Sire!" said the page, running into the throne room. In his hand he waved a piece of parchment. "I found this note pinned to the castle entrance."

"What does it say?"

"I don't know, your majesty. I can't read." He thrust the note in the king's face, but he too pushed it away. The king was a good and righteous man, but he could not read either. This story happened long ago, when reading was not as common as it is today. "Give it to the prince!" said the king, for the prince had been studying with a distant sorcerer.

The prince, who was still a young man, took the parchment in hand. The room fell silent as he agonized over the letters – reading was still very new to him. "Um...um," he stammered, the paper crinkling in his hands. "What does it say!" bellowed the king.

"I think, I think..." said the prince, beginning to sound out the letters. Everyone leaned a little closer. "I think it says, I...w-will...I will...be...thay, no there... I-will-be-there..."

"I will be there?" shouted the king. "Who? Who!" The king was a little excitable.

"Hold on," said the prince. "I will be there...in two da – days! I will be there in two days!"

"He'll be here in two days? Who? For goodness, sake! Is there a name on the parchment?"

"Hold on," said the prince, "here it is. It's signed at the bottom." Once again, all the king's knights and courtiers leaned close. "It's signed by...the...the...Ur-ay-nn-gee...Ka-nig-hit...The Urangee Kanighit!"

"The Urangee Kanighit?" said one of the knights with a horrible expression on his face. "What, God save us, is that?"

Everyone in the room looked around. The Urangee Kanighit? Must be some sort of monster, some giant hairy beast bent on destroying the castle and eating the children. Despair hung on everyone's expression. Their faces went white, and the bravest knight of all tried to tiptoe out the back, till the king, being the king, smacked the armored guard on his right with the back of his hand – bo-oi-ong – and slammed his fist on the table. "We're no cowards," he said. "Men, get your gear. I want every available horseman to head for the black forest as soon as possible. We must find..." and here he drew out the words with menace in his voice, "The Urangee Kanighit."

Silence. Then suddenly, everyone in the room was jostling for gear, a last bite of food, a word with the king, and finally for the door. The young prince went up to his father. "Father," he said, "I should go too. I must hunt for...The Urangee Kanighit."

"No, son," said the king, "you must stay safe behind the castle walls. Who knows what manner of beast this cursed Urangee Kanighit might be. Three heads. Fifteen legs. Half a dozen swords. He might be a ghost for all we know..." He paused, then shook his head. "No, we can't risk it. You're staying here with me."

The king's word was final. The prince hung his head and walked out of the room, servants and half-dressed knights clanging through the hallways.

All that day and the next morning, the king's knights searched for any trace of The Urangee Kanighit. "Must be ten feet high," said one man. "Arms the size of canons," said another. Truth is, every single one of them was terrified. But nobody found a thing.

Late in the afternoon of the second day, the young prince, bravery and fortune in his heart, slipped on the armor of a third-class knight and headed to the stables. "Ay, who is that?" said the stable master. "I thought all you men were out by now. Oh well, you're going to have to do with old Hobbledy-Peg, you will. I have no more horses but he."

"That'll do," said the prince in the huskiest voice he could muster. The stable master paused and cocked his ear, then shook it off and headed for old Hobbledy-Peg's stable. When he came out, the horse was limping with every third step, but it managed to walk up to the prince. "You best be quick," said the stable master. "The king won't look kindly on a latecomer."

It took longer than the prince had hoped to reach the woods, but by evening he was well into the black forest. Moss and lichens hung from the branches like the hair of old witches. Strange smells seemed to ooze out of the ground, and the horse's hobbled trot sounded as if it were ringing on hollow ground. Soon, the prince was terrified. He had made a mistake. There was no way he was going to find The Urangee Kanighit, and even if he did, what would he do? The monster would probably kill him in one blow. He called his horse to a stop. He began to turn around, then suddenly froze. There, not more than a hundred yards from him came a mysterious orange glow.

"Whoa," said the prince softly to his horse. But the horse didn't listen. It continued turning, the metal stirrups and rings of the saddle jingling like an old Christmas tree. The prince, terrified, kept his eyes on the glow. It must be the Urangee Kanighit, he thought, some sort of chimaera, a fiery beast with a snake's head and thick, black claws. It was drawing closer. "Rear," whispered the boy to the horse, the command to walk backwards, but the horse's legs had begun to shake. The prince also began to shake, and the two made a frightful clanging noise. The entire forest began to glow with an unnerving light, and in a last ditch of courage the prince opened his visor and shouted in his meanest voice, "Halt! Who goes there!" which didn't sound very mean.

Out from behind the trees came... The Orange Knight? The king's old friend? It couldn't be.

"Ah, young prince," said the wise old knight.

"Wha?" said the Prince, too bewildered to speak. "You're not...the what...are you..." Then he pulled himself together and asked, "Where's the Urangee Kanighit?"

"The Urangee Kanighit?" laughed the kindly knight. "What's that?"

"The Urangee Kanighit," said the prince. "It's supposed to be some kind of monster. It sent a note to my father saying that it was coming today to destroy the castle and eat all the children."

"The children?" asked the Orange Knight, chuckling to himself, "Sounds terrible." Then he added, "Did the note come on a piece of parchment?"

"It did."

"Did it say: I will be there in two days?"

"It did!"

"Who read it?" asked the knight.

"I did," said the boy. "Father can't read."

The Orange Knight roared a powerful laugh. "Oh, son," he said, "we're gonna have a good time together." He squeezed the young prince's shoulder, then took the reins of old Hobbledy-Peg and the two headed toward the castle.

By the time I finished the last few lines of this story with my students, they were rolling on the ground and pressing themselves into the walls with laughter. Honestly, it was mayhem – like a cartoon show where they're taking off their shoes and hitting themselves on the head. When we finally came to our senses, I went over a few details on the board. The Urangee Kanighit. The Orange Knight. What a bunch of ridiculous nonsense. Now, we use it as a catch-all to explain why, as we learn to read, there are words that break the rules and simply don't make sense. We can call these words "sight words" and develop all kinds of methods to learn them, but now we have a fun way to encounter these oddities in school. We can laugh it off and capture the entire message in six syllables – Urangee Kanighit. The levity this brings to schoolwork is priceless.

Stories for the Whole Family

If we grasp that relationship is at the center of storytelling, we can apply its balm almost anywhere, not just with children. In this chapter, we invite you to explore storytelling as an activity for the whole family, the neighborhood, or any gathering.

Storytelling is a great activity for inter-generational bonding. This can be as simple as a story from mother, father, and child, but can easily include grandparents, aunts, uncles, cousins, or neighbors. A story circle like this can be a very intimate gathering. Young children benefit from listening to elders' stories, and elders benefit from listening to children's stories. In a circle of multiple ages, we have a chance to see life in all its aspects, and personality in its myriad forms. As with the one-on-one moments of storytelling, the primary focus is connection. By giving our full attention to each speaker, we receive something much more profound than the narratives. We share a common bond that has deep roots with our human ancestors, something that is hard to replicate with the unidirectional focus of a movie or TV show, no matter how magnificent the screenplay.

Calling such a circle into being will take some courage. Most adults don't think of themselves as storytellers. Why? Because we're focused on narrative. We tend to grow shy and noncommittal. This is why having children in your circle can make a big difference, because adults tend to show up for kids in ways we normally wouldn't for other adults, like a round of hokey-pokey. Once the ice is broken, we usually have a lot of fun.

To begin, find a spot that is comfortable for everyone, either a quiet space inside or maybe under a favorite tree. Be sure that elders have a good place to sit, and that everyone can see one another. It should be clear that when someone is speaking, everyone else is listening. This may need to be vocalized at the outset. Interruptions from outside voices can derail someone taking a risk, and we want to create an environment where people feel welcome and comfortable. You might begin by telling a brief story yourself, then inviting the person to your left or right to tell one, and so on. The first two stories are usually the hardest, so choose your speakers wisely, but by the third or so people will usually begin to grasp the value of the moment. It will be utterly unique every time.

Another method to try is to have everyone tell a common story. One person begins, then passes the story to the next. That person develops the story a little further, then passes it along. As we watch common characters travel through the lips of different storytellers, we have a chance to see personality in its myriad ages and forms. Some will lose the story. Others will win it back. Sometimes, a sentence or two is enough. Often, the most enjoyable moments are the gaffs and goofs.

A regular gathering like this – even if it's just once a year at grandma's house – can have a major impact on the intimacy of the group as a whole. It's been said that a family that prays together stays together. Perhaps we might say that a family that tells stories together grows old together. Instead of game night or movie night, try a story night. See how it goes. Experiment.

Some adults, especially the coolest ones, will hesitate to enter such a diverse story circle. It can feel extremely vulnerable. In a world where cynicism and aloofness are often valued, it is very hard to pull playfulness out of some adults. Sometimes, the only way we can do that is through children's activities. The truth is that everything mentioned in this book works for adults too, but most will not choose to go there unless the ante is upped by the inclusion of kids. This is partly how kids "teach" the adults. They sometimes are the only window into the inner child of the gruffest character.

For those of us willing to take a little more risk, we might find the same kind of intimacy generated when there are no children involved at all. After all, storytelling is already a common part of every adult gathering. It's just not called storytelling. It's called, "Oh my goodness, let me tell you what happened when…" The trading of tales is as old as taverns, markets, and the office coffee pot. Why? Because telling stories creates intimacy.

Silke had an elderly friend, Mary, living with terminal cancer. In the months before her death, she was fully alert, but no longer able to walk much farther than a few steps outside her home. Soon, she was bedridden. When Silke visited, the two friends basked in their common love, but the gravity of the situation made it so that common banter felt pedantic. "Tell me a story," Mary often said.

In the last chapter, we mentioned how stories are uniquely useful for parents and educators who want to teach important lessons without generating the one-on-one positionality that sometimes brings conflict or discomfort. This same quality is at play in a variety of circumstances, like Silke's visits with Mary. Storytelling removes the awkwardness of saying or repeating something that isn't needed. We can simply be held in the intimacy of the story, without any practical agenda.

This quality is so subtle, yet so diverse, that it can be used almost anywhere. You might try using it the next time you want to send a message that you know will land a little roughly. No one likes being told that they did something wrong, even if they agree. It's simply human nature to grow defensive. The result is that, even when both parties are in agreement about the error, much of our focus goes toward the power struggle and any lingering irritation. This is positionality at work. But if you couch that message in a story – thirty seconds is often enough – the person has an opportunity to discover the error for himself. This mitigates lingering discomfort between parties. Leaders who have mastered this technique are mind-blowing. They are capable of critiquing their employees, students, followers, etc., while simultaneously fostering their goodwill.

A good place to try this storytelling technique is with your husband or wife. You might use it to deliver an important message in a gentle way, as described above, but you can also use it as a way to generate connection and intimacy with your partner. It works just like it works with your child. If your relationship is like most people's, you probably have some dull stretches. Next time you're in bed at the end of the day, rehashing what happened at work or at home, and perhaps finding it a little difficult to create common ground, stop. Tell a story. Invest in it. Be real. Be loving. See what happens.

This works best if you have your partner's cooperation. It is like a small, intimate storytelling circle, and you might both take a moment to tell a story. When it's your turn, give yourself fully to it. Use the storytelling loop – take something from your day that you and your partner will recognize into your story, add some whimsical or fascinating details, and then close the loop by bringing it back to reality. Notice if anything changes. When it's your turn to listen, give your presence just as fully to your partner as you would to your child. Listen with all your heart. Doing this just once a week can be transformative, because, once again, it takes the one-on-one pressure off your encounters. The intimacy you build can be folded into the rest of your days.

You might try starting a story, then asking your partner to finish it. Experiment. Find what works. If you believe your partner will laugh the suggestion off, consider taking your first dive into storyland without any preparation. A story is usually more powerful than an explanation of why stories are powerful. Next time you notice the two of you struggling to connect, you might just take a leap and start with, "Once upon a time…"

To the novice, some of these suggestions will sound absurd. At the very least, they will sound difficult to achieve. But if we begin with simple stories, usually through the lens of childhood, the average adult will have little trouble applying the techniques described in these last chapters. It will become almost second-nature to reach out to a traumatized child and defuse some of their pain with a soothing story. It will be surprisingly easy to create fun and engaging stories that send home important messages to our kids about growing up. We may be able to cut off arguments with our partners before they explode. If we're lucky, we will grasp that storytelling is an evolved human adaptation that efficiently conveys information and builds intimacy, giving us a useful tool for nurturing relationships with friends, family and neighbors of all ages.

Practice #14 – Tell a Story to a Friend

The purpose of this exercise is to tell a story to an adult. Find a friend or loved one that feels safe. Invite them to spend thirty minutes or an hour with you. If you like, share a word or two about why you wish to do this. Maybe the ideas in this book will help you explain. But don't get caught up in the explanation. Try to dive right in. If possible, use the storytelling loop to keep an anchor in the real world. When you're done, give your friend an opportunity to tell a story. When you've both finished, take a moment to acknowledge what you liked and perhaps what was uncomfortable. Be careful not to criticize your friend's story.

Practice #15 – Tell a Story to an Enemy

This exercise is for the bold. Find someone in your life where the relationship feels strained. Maybe this is a coworker, another parent at school, or whoever. Don't make a huge thing of it, but when the opportunity strikes, try to tell this person a short story, one that is largely uplifting. Make it simple and easy for you, so that you don't fear it. It does not have to be some wild fanciful tale from the imagination. It might just be something that happened to you that seems relevant at this moment. It doesn't need to be longer than a minute. Afterward, notice how you feel.

Sample Story – A Christmas Story

By Silke Rose West & Joseph Sarosy

It was Christmas Eve, and as the sun dipped below the horizon a number of cars had begun to arrive. There was a fire in the pit and tealights along the walkways. The mountains receded into the shadows and the air was cold, but hot cider warmed our lips and hands. After lighting red candles on our outdoor Christmas tree, an amusing and dangerous task, Silke invited everyone to a story circle.

You could see the expressions. A few of them lit up. Some shrugged. Most were masked in polite smiles that meant they were nervous. One child beamed, another hid behind a parent's leg. Truth is, most of us were strangers, known to Silke through various means. There were young adults, the kind that show up with drums and soft voices, bent on a rollicking, good-natured holiday. There were parents intent on celebrating Christmas Eve without all the stuff. There were elders, and a family from out of town whose son had attended Silke's kindergarten twenty-odd years ago.

"Here's how it works," Silke said in her kindergarten voice, a mischievous smile on her face. "One of us starts the story, then passes it to the next person. You tell as much as you like, then pass it on. We'll go around the circle, and I think we'll know when we're done."

"We just want to hear a story from you," said one of the adults. A few people laughed.

"I'll start," said a young woman, accustomed to this kind of thing. Everyone turned their eyes to her, and she began. "There was once a Christmas fairy, and she had come to help deliver gifts for all the people. But along the way, she got lost."

We waited for second, but it was clear she was done. She looked kindly to the man next to her, a middle-aged man in loafers and a jacket much too thin for an outdoor event like this. His hands stuffed firmly in his pockets, he looked left and right, then said, "There was a hole. She fell in it." A couple chuckles rippled through the crowd.

The man's wife was next, and she had a vivid expression on her face as she picked up the story, maybe a little too eagerly. "Inside the hole, she looked for a way to get out. It was very dark, so she felt along the edges."

"Can't fairies fly?" someone asked. A couple people snickered. Two eyeballs glared at her. One man scraped the toe of his shoe over the ground. But most of the circle kept their eyes on the storyteller in a show of support. By and large, this was a gentle group.

"Suddenly, she found a door. Um, well, at first she didn't know it was a door, but she could feel the wood. She knocked, and it sounded hollow. So, she reached down and opened the door."

There was a brief pause as the demure man next to the speaker picked up the story. Another kindergarten teacher, this man had probably logged several thousand story-hours prior to this event.

You could hear it in his voice, his delivery, and the way each sentence lit up the story like a person walking through a house turning on lamps. He kept his eyes down the entire time, but by the time he was done, we had some real meat to work with.

"She opened the door into a large room. On one side was a pile of presents wrapped in colorful paper, and on the other side was a white staircase that led out of the room. When she looked back the way she had come in, the door had disappeared. Hanging on the wall was a small key. She reached for the key, but every time her hand drew near, the key moved away so that she could never grasp it. She grew frustrated and sat down. There was a small table nearby and on top of it was a handwritten note."

Now, people were curious. The man who had been dragging his toe in the dirt looked intently at the speaker. Everyone was eager for him to go on, but instead he turned and looked kindly on the child to his right. After catching his eye, she tucked her head to her chin and winced in a joyful expression of nervousness. She looked back at the man, then the ground, then into the circle of faces eager to hear what the child would make of it. "She read the note, and it said to go up the stairs."

"Mm-hm," said an old woman, a small show of support.

"Very good," said another, a little heavy on the praise.

The young girl was eyeballing the woman next to her, a twenty-something who had earlier replaced every mention of Christmas with the word solstice. She gazed with wide eyes at the little girl, then turned to the crowd. "With the note in hand, she headed for the stairs. When she put her foot on the first step, it turned red. She paused for a second in wonder, then took another step. This one turned orange. The next was yellow, green, silver, blue, purple and gold. She kept climbing, and the stairs turned every color of the rainbow and she saw magical flowers growing all alongside the stairs. It filled her with magic and wonder, and she kept climbing till she looked over the staircase and saw a wonderful rainbow with every sort of color and shape springing from the staircase."

Certain she had improved the story dramatically, she passed the story to the right. A tall man with a bit of a belly stood with tightly pressed lips. "The candles are going out!" someone yelled. We all turned, and sure enough, of the twenty or so candles on the tree, only three were now lit. Silke and another woman relit a few, which promptly blew out, then gave up and returned to the circle. This distraction had given plenty of time for the pot-bellied man to grow exceedingly uncomfortable. Suddenly, all eyes were back on him.

"Well," he said, sticking his lips out in an expression of thoughtfulness, "when she got to the top, the little Christmas fairy realized she was on the top of the rainbow. The sky above was dark, and she could see that the moon and stars were quite near. Stretching as tall as she could, she reached her hand out and plucked one of the stars from the sky." Pleasantly surprised, the circle seemed to smile in approval.

Next, an impish man who happens to be writing this book, a little grossed out by the saccharine quality of the story, began. *"When she looked down at the rainbow, everything had gone black and white. Suddenly, she felt sad. She wasn't even sure why. Maybe it had something to do with the star, but she didn't know. She tried to put it back, but it wouldn't stick. Slowly, she walked back down the staircase, wondering where all the color had gone. By the time she got to the bottom, her heart was heavy. It was hard to imagine delivering presents. Besides, she was stuck in some underground hole. She had to find a way out."*

"She took the star to the key," said the next woman. *"As she walked across the room, she could see that the presents had gone black and white too. Everything in the room was a little gloomy, but she wanted to do something about it. When she got to the key, it jumped off the wall and stuck to the star like a magnet."*

Now, it was Silke's turn. *"The little girl, whoops, I mean the little fairy, held the star key in her hand and put it where the door had been. Suddenly, she could see it. The key fit into the lock, and with one turn the door opened with a click."*

Silke turned to the old woman next to her. Everyone could see that she was nervous. *"I don't...I'm just not..."* she said, looking with pleading eyes toward Silke.

"I know!" said the young man next to her. *"When the door opened, the presents lit up with color."* The old woman looked at the

young man, grateful to have some help. "Yes," she said, "and the fairy put them all in a little bag."

"A velvet bag," said the young man.

"A red velvet bag," said the old woman, looking pleased.

"She carried the red velvet bag, which was very heavy, out the door, but she was feeling much lighter and happier. When she looked back, the rainbow staircase was once more colorful and bright."

The young man and the old woman smiled, then turned to the child to their right.

"She climbed out the hole and delivered all the presents," said the child.

"And when she got home," said the child's mother, "she reached in her pocket and found the star. It was her own little Christmas gift."

We all smiled. The story had reached its natural conclusion just as it came back to its starting point in the circle. It was sappy. It was a little trite, but it didn't really matter. It had brought us together as people. Strangers beforehand, we all walked away from that circle with something more in our hearts. Soon, we had dissolved in different directions, some to the fire, some for cider, others walking the half-lit paths. The Christmas tree had one candle softly glowing on its branches.

The purpose of a story circle isn't so much the story. It's the shared intimacy.

The End

When you first picked up this book, you might have thought that storytelling was about telling playful stories to children. It is, but we hope that you now see storytelling as something richer, a unique human tool to share information and foster intimacy throughout a person's entire life.

We already know this, if unconsciously. People are captivated by stories, and have been since the dawn of *Homo sapiens*. We have literally evolved, as Brian Boyd, Jonathan Gottschall, and many others have suggested, into storytellers and listeners. Far from being extraneous, storytelling is a highly useful tool used to garner social attention, simulate difficult experiences, and disseminate essential information. Aside from our direct senses, our brains are wired to receive information most readily through story. It is the primary method by which we pass on family, religious and cultural values. It is how we make meaning of our lives.

From the moment we wake up till the moment we go to bed, we are frequently listening to or telling stories.

We might not call it storytelling, but the majority of the words we say or hear are wrapped in the container of story. When we retire at night, our brains continue to tell us stories as we sleep. In fact, we are so saturated with story that we sometimes have a hard time recognizing it, like the proverbial woodsman not being able to see the forest for the trees.

The number of videos, movies and books now available to the average child makes it so that stories pervade a child's life perhaps more than ever before. Some of those stories are good. Some of them are bad. But there's no question that many of them are highly engrossing. The result is that many parents, most of whom themselves grew up within this media saturation, are rightly intimidated by storytelling. We might know a handful of teachers or friends we think of as good storytellers, but in the face of giants like HBO and Disney, we count ourselves out.

If we look at storytelling as merely the passing on of a narrative, then this position is tenable. Most of us don't have the imaginative power to compete with *Frozen*. So, why try? It might be true that *Frozen* outshines our humble Little Bear stories, but if we begin to see that storytelling is about the relationship between speaker and listener, we open a window to a new perspective. A child who has grown up with the intimacy of story time does not have a hard time differentiating a parent's stories from the kinds of stories he finds elsewhere. He will likely prefer them in many contexts. In any case, there won't be much need for comparison, because both parent and child will recognize and feel the difference.

The purpose of this book is to inspire parents and caregivers to take possession of the storytelling tradition that rightfully belongs to us as human beings. Partly, this is to provide our children with the engrossing stories that only arise from within the intimacy of family, but we also wish to encourage parents to recapture the joy that comes from this uniquely creative expression. It is not merely a question of whom or what our child is paying attention to, but what outlets we have created for ourselves to express the intimacy, joy and seriousness that we find in our day to day lives. Storytelling is not a one-way street. It's about the whole relationship.

The first step is to be yourself. This is your foundation, and it's worth taking some time to get it right. Otherwise, the relationship you're building with your child is with someone you're only pretending to be. Don't build a mansion on a shaky foundation. It may turn out to be a house of cards.

The next step is to start simple. This is most easily done if your child is still young. There's good reason to start at the first day of your child's life, but try not to wait longer than three or four years of age. This makes it easy, and helps develop your routine. The most important aspect of your storytelling routine is simply doing it. Storytelling takes practice. You will have bad days, and bad stories. We still do all the time. But if you have a regular routine, the intimacy of the moment will outshine any goofs.

If you use the storytelling loop, your stories will be not only imaginative, but constantly tied back into your child's real world. This creates outlets for play and memory, and in time it can lead to very rich story environments where many dolls, toys, places, objects and activities remind your child of your time together and prompt her to further creative outlets for play.

By using descriptive language and some of the other storytelling techniques described in Nuts and Bolts, you can add richness and depth to your stories. If you keep a regular practice, your child will give you cues, and you will find that your stories mature, often almost effortlessly.

This alone will create immeasurably rich experiences, regular moments of shared meaning, and lifelong memories that you and your child will treasure. But once we've gotten our story legs under us, we can add further layers of meaning and richness to our lives, soothing, teaching, and bringing the intimacy of storytelling into all of our relationships. At the close of life, just as at the beginning, there is often a renewed interest in the power of a simple story. There is no end.

Practice #16 – Listen to Your Story

Each of us carries an internal story of who we are. We are beautiful, strong, smart, athletic, dumb, bad, a victim and more. What stories have been pervasive in your life? Are they true? How and when did those stories develop? What can you do now to shepherd healthy stories into your child's mind and heart?

Practice #17 – Listen to Your Child's Story

Invite your child to tell you a story. Listen for the themes, images and feelings that arise. Don't be quick to judge. Just observe. If the exercise is fruitful, consider making it a regular part of story time, and try to pay attention to consistent images or themes that come up for your child.

Sample Story – Butterflies

By Joseph Sarosy

It was almost the last day of school. The river was high and the earth was green. Silke, the children, and I had been in the forest building homes out of sticks and branches. As we did, hundreds of butterflies flew about us, suckling at white flowers that hung on the wild currants. Now it was time for lunch, and as we settled into the shade, Silke and I began exchanging glances, as if to say you? Me?

I smiled and shook my head. Butterflies. That's all we needed. After the kids finished their lunches, they zipped up their packs, looked for a comfy spot, and took on the posture of story. We had been through this countless times.

"Alright," I said, once the movement had settled. "I'm going to tell you a story. It's about a grub." I made a face, meaning I'm sorry, *then shrugged my shoulders. "You know what a grub is? It's basically a worm. That's all it is. Kind'a wiggly and squinchy. This grub's name was Gertie. Gertie the grub.*

"Well, Gertie loved to eat. She liked to eat grass and leaves and stuff, but she was born in the fall. She ate as much as she could, but soon there wasn't anything left to eat. She was a bit sad. Not knowing what else to do, she climbed into a hole in a tree and sort'a snuggled up. Outside the window, she watched as the green earth became brown and dry. She became awfully sleepy. Once, she woke up and everything was white. And cold."

"It was winter," one of the kids said, "snow."

"Mm-hm, that's right. Winter. Pfft, *it was cold as a moldy-rolder. Cold as a shoulder boulder. I mean it was* cold, *and Gertie just didn't know what to do, 'cept sleep. So, that's what she did. Zzzzz…."* I closed my eyes and made snoring noises a la The Three Stooges. *A few kids laughed. Some mimicked me. I laughed too. Silke smiled. The forest. I could do this forever.*

"Well, one day, Gertie woke up." *I looked left and right, feigning seriousness.* Sniff-sniff. "Something was different. She peered out the hole and saw the bright sun. I don't know why, but for some reason she decided to climb out the little window, the little hole that was in the tree. Oh! *It was green. Everywhere. The bushes had green shoots coming out of the branches. The grasses were growing green on the dry stalks from last year. And it was loud! Gertie looked and saw the rushing river, high from all the melted snow. And the trees. My goodness, the trees. Well, Gertie took one look and her mouth started to drool like a big ol' Labrador. A dog. Tongue hangin' out and all. She climbed down, found a branch.* Mm! *The eatin' was good."*

"Well, Gertie's sittin' on the branch, munchin' away when all of a sudden she sees a branch on the other side of the bush, sort'a bobbin'." *I turned my own head to the side, as if peering over a branch. Silence. I turned the other way, trying to get a view.* "She looked. But she couldn't see anything, so she went back to eating. Well, she's sittin' there eating, and the branch is bobbing, and she looked." *Again, I peered over the imaginary branches. Nothing.*

"Well, she decided to walk over there and see what's up. She wiggled along, you know, the way a grub's gotta do it, more belly than foot, and finally she makes her way to the other branch. Bobbing.

"Well, there's Greg. Greg is another grub, just like Gertie. And Gertie's like, 'Whatch'a doin'?'

"'Me?' says Greg, mouth all stuffed with leaves and drippy juices.

"'Yeah,' says Gertie.

"'Oh, I'm just eatin' leaves. You know. Chillin'.'

"'Mm-hm,' says Gertie, 'I know how that is.'

"'Yep.'

"Well, now they's good friends. Gertie and Greg. And the whole forest is getting greener and greener and greener. Pfft! I'm talkin' grub heaven.

I'll pause for a second to state the obvious, which is that, so far, pretty much nothing has happened. The story is as boring as could be. But the kids were in seventh heaven. I was making funny voices, pausing and acting weird, and they ate it up for the same reason I did. We're friends. It hardly mattered what the story was. It is enough to eat lunch under a shady tree and listen to someone you trust. Besides, they know my stories. They knew it would get somewhere. Anticipation can be sweet.

"Finally, one day Gertie gets tired. I mean real tired. She's like, whoa, I can hardly keep my head up. She's all floppy. So, and now she doesn't know why, but she's just like, I'm a hang on this branch." I shrugged my shoulders, then spoke in a different tone. "Come on, Gertie. Whatch'a doin'? But Gertie's not listenin'. She's just doin' her thing."

"Well…" I dropped my voice low, growing serious. "Guys. I mean, Gertie doesn't even know what's happening. She falls asleep and as she does it's like her whole body becomes stiff. It's hard, like a shell. She's just hangin' there, not moving. But inside," and my eyes opened wide. "Inside, it's like her whole body has gone soft. It's like…it's like oatmeal in there. Mushy and warm. I don't know what's going on, guys, but it's like the wildest magic you've ever seen. I'm talkin' Gertie is a hard thing on a branch and a soft thing inside and I don't even know where Gertie is anymore. That's how it is, and it's that way for a long time. And as she's sleeping, she has a dream." I paused, a stony, serious expression on my face.

"You know what happened in that dream?" A few kids shook their heads. I shook mine left and right, as if I wished I didn't have to tell it.

"Well, check this out. Gertie is in the forest and she meets a fairy. Fairies fly, so that's cool. The fairy comes down and she says, 'I have a very important message for you, Gertie. You have a big job to do.' Well, Gertie's a little nervous, but she's listening. 'Gertie,' says the fairy, and she's real serious, 'when you wake up, Mother Earth has asked that you watch over the kids and keep them safe.' Gertie stared as the fairy flew away."

"Kc.... *Gertie wakes up. It's like she's been away for months. Or years. But really, it's only been a few weeks. The sound that woke her, that crack, was her own body. You know what I'm sayin'? Her own body.* Crack, *you know?*

"*Whew, she's sleepy. She's scared. Finally, she yawns and s-t-r-e-t-c-h-e-s her arms,*" and here I mimed these motions. "*And it... hold on, somethin' ain't right. She looks at her arms, and then she's like, wait a minute, I didn't have arms before. But now her arms are, well, they ain't arms no more.*" All the kids turned and looked at each other. She's a butterfly, *they said with their eyes.*

"*Well, she stretches her arms out, which are now wings, and she's sort'a soggy and wet. She's just hanging, kind'a wakin' up, drying off, gathering her attention. She looks into the world, and it's even greener than before. The grasses are totally green now, and the bushes aren't just green. Guys, wow, they're covered in flowers. The trees are big and leafy and shady. The river is burbling, a little quieter than it was before. Gertie's awake. Now, she remembers. She's back. She sees the bushes. She's beautiful. She's strong.*

"*Well, she's sittin' on the branch, hanging really, and she sees something. The branch on the other side is, well, sort'a bobbin'. She turns to look. Then to the other side. She can't tell what it is.* Sniff-sniff. *Smells good, though. She looks again. Branch is bobbing. It's not clear. Well, she decides to walk over, but as she does* – pwooh!

"*Her whole body lifts into the air. And as she draws her arms into herself, it's...it's... Well, she's flying. It's the most wonderful* thing she's ever done. She's just floating on the wind, circling, spinning. It's like the wind is moving her, but she's moving the wind. It's just amazing. Well, she sees the branch, and by pulling on her arms a little bit, she glides down and lands. There's flowers all over it, little hanging white flowers, and it smells incredible. She looks, pfft!, and she laughs. It's Greg! He's hanging on that branch and he's crawling out of something.

"'Greg!,' she says, 'where you been?'

"'Me?' says Greg, sort'a wide eyed. 'Wait, hold on,' he says. He opened one of his wings, then folded it back. 'Gertie. I had the most amazing dream. I was sleeping, and then this fairy came to me. She said I have to do something.'" The kids started eyeing each other again.

"'Really?' said Gertie. 'I had a dream too. Did she...was it...'

"'The kids,' said Greg, 'I'm supposed to watch the kids...'

"'And keep them safe?' said Gertie. 'Greg, I had the same dream.'"

I could see the round lips of intelligent surprise forming on the children's faces. We were all in on it now. Me, Silke, Gertie, the kids, Greg. The forest.

"Well, you know what happens. They's butterflies now. Gertie and Greg, flying around. Big, wild currant bushes everywhere. It's just. The whole world is full of bushes and flowers and food, and it's just so good, and so delicious. And I mean, you know, they're flyin' around and there's like, hundreds, maybe thousands of these little butterflies everywhere. And there's kids. And the kids come through, and the butterflies are flying around, and they're watchin'. You know? They're watchin' the kids, keeping 'em safe. That's just how it is. And it goes on like that for a long time. Butterflies. Kids. Chillin'. It's good stuff."

I stopped. The kids looked up. They could hear the end of the story in the tone of my voice.

It's easy to doubt the power of this story. It's a little saccharine for some, too much street lingo for others. I don't suggest you do it this way. It's just my way. It's who I am. I like being silly and giving the children overt reasons to doubt me. It makes them giggle, and it gives them permission to question my words. They get to decide for themselves whether there is any lasting truth to the story. I hope you feel the same when you read this book. Storytelling belongs to you. The method we've described gives a helpful framework, but there's room within it for as many different expressions as there are people on the planet.

As the children emerged from rest time into that field of butterflies, their eyes lit up. The butterflies flitted about much the same. The currant bushes hadn't changed. There was even reason to doubt teacher's silly story. But the truth wasn't exactly the point. It was enough for the children to have heard the idea and wonder, even if only for a moment, whether a field of butterflies was actually keeping them safe. Or, perhaps it was enough to draw a little boy's attention to the very real butterflies that earlier in the day he had ignored. What was unquestionably real, however, was the palpable sense of community felt amongst the children, the shared joy on their faces, and the loving presence of the teachers as we emerged from the trees into that field of butterflies. It wasn't just make-believe.

The Storytelling Loop

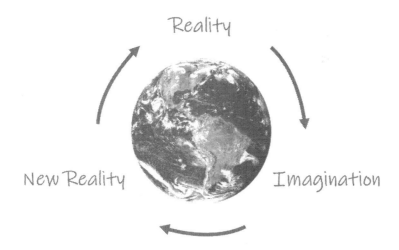

Reality

New Reality

Imagination

Our Goal

Our goal is to help parents, educators and caregivers use storytelling to create lasting intimacy with their children. We hope this book inspired you. If you have not yet started telling stories, we invite you to take the plunge and begin today. Nothing will develop your craft better than regular practice. The exercises listed at the end of each chapter are a good place to start, but we invite you to follow your heart as well. This skill is something that lies deep inside you. You will know when you are on the right track.

There is, of course, a lot more to storytelling than we've put into this book. Our intention was to create a short read for busy parents, with a simple method and memorable steps. Have we done that? We'd love to hear from you.

www.howtotellstoriestochildren.com
facebook.com/howtotellstoriestochildren

Best of Luck! *Silke & Joe*

Acknowledgements

This book is the work of many storytellers. Thanks to all the children who have been a part of our storytelling years. Thanks to the Gnomes, the Earth Children, and all the teachers and parents who have crossed our paths. Thank you to our own children, to our parents, and to our unknown ancestors that made this gift possible.

We are especially indebted to Alison P Brown, Amy W. Hope, Andrea B, Angela Prettie, Angelika Heikaus, Ayesha Candy Cruz, Beth Gallatin, Brandon Hubley & Jolie & Diedre & Nancy & Karleen & Matthew & Caroline & Jean, Brock Anderson, Chase & Rachel & Aldo Stearnes, Damon McLean, Dan Brodnik, Dana Klepper-Smith, Daniel Lodwig, Danielle Avdul, Danielle Freeman, Devin Powell, Diana Rico, Diane Singerman, Ed Neal & Sue Lewis, Emily Kedar, Emma Avalos & Seth Blowers, Erinn Kilcullen, Francis Scully, Freya Markowski, Gilbert Renault, Glen Carlberg, Grace Iverson, Inka Markowski, Irina Sels, Jai & Jan Cross, Jared Krause, Jenn Foley, Jenny Kostecki-Shaw & Patrick Shaw, Jessica & Matt Jones, Joe Plummer, Joseph and Michelena Mcpherson, Kara Andresen, Karen Moravek, Katy McKay, Kendra Adler, Larry Wiesner, Lindsay E. Nance, Loretta Neal, Lou & Jane Brodnik, Malinda, Marcy Andrew, Margaret Brewster, Marie Goodwin, Mark Dixon, Mari Tara, Matthew Ryan, Michele Boccia, Michelle Williams, Mike Pumphrey, Mirabai Starr & Ganga Das Little, Nancy McDaniel, Paola Marusich, Paul Rudy, Paul Wapner, Peter Brodnik, Philip & Patricia Cummings, Rachael Penn, Rae Halder, Renay Anderson, Renee Angele Mason, Roberta Sharples, Ron Boyd, Sally A Boyd, Samantha Brody, Satyadev, Sena Rasun-Mahendra, Sevenup, Stuart Stein, Tracy Cates, and Zwanet Hamming.

Thank you to Jenny Kostecki-Shaw for the beautiful cover image and for helping with the design. Thank you to Bridget Wagner Matzie for helping us shape the book into something meaningful.

Made in the USA
Columbia, SC
19 January 2020

86946956R00083